SERVICE AND SELLING

Mark Blumsky
with Neil Miller

Hodder Moa

To the Customer: sometimes you can be incredibly difficult and my shop will always be a lot tidier without you, but thanks, because without you I have a real problem

National Library of New Zealand Cataloguing-in-Publication Data
Blumsky, Mark, 1957-
Slippers : service & selling : what the plumber taught the mayor /
Mark Blumsky & Neil Miller.
ISBN 978-1-86971-158-0
1. Customer services. 2. Selling. 3. Business. 4. Management.
I. Miller, Neil. II. Title.
658—dc 22

A Hodder Moa Book
Published in 2009 by Hachette New Zealand Ltd
4 Whetu Place, Mairangi Bay
Auckland, New Zealand

Text © Mark Blumsky and Neil Miller 2009
The moral rights of the author have been asserted.

Design and format © Hachette New Zealand Ltd 2009

All rights reserved. No part of this publication may be reproduced or transmitted in any form or by any means, electronic or mechanical, including photocopying, recording, or any information storage and retrieval system, without permission in writing from the publisher.

Designed and produced by Hachette New Zealand Ltd
Printed by Griffin Press, Australia

Acknowledgements

I'd especially like to thank...

Neil, because if you hadn't had the energy and courage to put the first words down, we never would've got this far.

Rachel, your wisdom and feedback made a real difference to the final shape of the book.

Paul, your empathy with the story and your ability to help it flow was critical.

The Plumber: I needed a hero and you were it, and — damn it — I never did sell you any slippers.

Corinne and Kendra, for helping me find my slippers, and not getting cross at me when every so often I would lose them. Your support is just awesome.

Mark Blumsky

Finding your slippers

Starting and building a business can be a very lonely process.

I was fortunate enough to be able to draw on the lessons I learnt from a single encounter with a plumber. The conversation with him changed the way I looked at business and, indeed, at life. If I hadn't met the plumber, I probably wouldn't have started my own business or become a mayor and a Member of Parliament. It was one of those moments that open your eyes to opportunity and move you forward.

But it was a matter of luck, and not everybody gets that lucky. There are lots of books that claim to tell you how to succeed in business, but many tend to be dense, quite theoretical and not really an easy read.

Ideally, a business success book should be easy, accessible and reassuring, full of real-life experiences and illuminating anecdotes. It should be like having a mentor on your bookshelf who you can call on any time. It should be a friend. The other sort of book is more like the intimidating teacher who expected you to understand things first time round and got angry when you didn't.

Over the past seven years I've given many speeches in which I described how I came upon the 'slippers' concept and how it worked for me and for others. So many people came up to me afterwards to say that they made an instant connection with my message that I decided to develop and expand it into a book — a friendly book. This is the result.

It's not an autobiography. Rather, it's a collection of stories and experiences connected by the slippers theme. It's a distillation of what I've seen and learnt and put into practice, a guide to what I truly believe is a better way of doing business.

The challenge for businesses is to find their own slippers and to enjoy the process of implementing them. Many companies could be much better if they developed their slippers. Change is never easy, but in the long run choosing not to change is a far greater gamble. The business landscape is crowded with examples of people who didn't and don't stand up and stand out. So many lost opportunities.

It doesn't have to be that way.

Mark Blumsky
Wellington
January 2009

The biggest decision

When an experienced offshore operator with a strong track record lodged an application to build and operate a casino in Wellington, it triggered intense debate in the capital city.

Supporters and opponents agreed on one thing: it was a massive decision which would have a far-reaching impact on the city's development. Those in favour pointed to the economic benefits, particularly the jobs that would be created. They argued that Wellington was now a grown-up, worldly city and this type of entertainment was in increasing demand from the tourists whom the city was attracting in ever-greater numbers.

Those against were concerned about the costly social consequences of problem gambling, and they were vehemently opposed to allowing a monument to temptation to occupy a prime spot on the beautiful waterfront.

The Wellington City Council would have the final say. The clear-cut division of opinion in the community was reflected in the council chambers, where both points of view had passionate supporters around the council table.

As councillors finalised their positions amid intense lobbying, it became increasingly clear that the council was split right down the middle, meaning the casino proposal's fate would hang on the casting vote of Mayor Mark Blumsky. As the day of judgement approached, Mark grew uncomfortably aware that delivering the casting vote would be the easy part. The hard part would be explaining the reasons for his decision to the council and the people of Wellington.

The odds always favour the house

Most people expected Mark to vote for the casino. From the outset Mark himself had expected to vote for a casino.

What the plumber taught the mayor about business

His core philosophy was pro-business and pro-development and the economic impact assessment made a strong case for the casino, indicating that it would bring a great deal of money into the city and create lots of jobs.

Coming from a business background, Mark's instincts told him it was a no-brainer. The facts spoke for themselves; the economic advantages were clear-cut. Who in their right mind could ignore that level of potential economic benefit? However, he had to concede that he didn't know all that much about the casino industry. Before he cast his vote, he wanted to see first-hand how casinos impacted on the city and the community and talk to the people directly affected.

He jumped on a plane to Melbourne.

Melbourne's casino blew Mark away. It was everything he'd expected and much, much more: sumptuous, luxurious, buzzing with excitement, clean, vibrant. He loved the dramatic architecture, the glitzy shows and the dazzling light displays. He was astonished at the size of the crowds who swarmed in to try their luck and the numbers of staff needed to keep the action humming and the punters happy around the clock.

And when he walked out of the casino, the knock-on effect was immediately apparent: new shops, hotels, bars and restaurants had sprung up in the immediate vicinity and were doing a roaring trade housing, feeding and watering casino patrons. When he talked to the proprietors of these new businesses, they made no bones about the fact that they were on the pig's back and were quick to credit the casino as the driver of the district's spectacular growth.

The turn of the card

Although dazzled by the pyrotechnics he'd witnessed and impressed by the way the casino was acting as a growth engine for the surrounding area, Mark decided to take a break from the bright lights and full-on action. Holidaying in Melbourne a few years earlier, before the casino had opened, he'd stumbled across a great little shopping precinct. It was a twenty-minute walk away so he could kill two birds with one stone: get in some gentle exercise while he absorbed what he'd seen.

With each city block he put between himself and the casino, Mark noticed there was less of a buzz on the streets. There weren't many people around, but there were plenty of boarded-up shops and 'for rent' signs. Tourists were conspicuous by their absence and the few locals didn't seem full of the joys of spring. This wasn't the vibrant shopping area he remembered from his previous visit.

He went looking for the menswear shop where he'd bought some of his favourite ties. It was still there, but the atmosphere had changed. The previously bubbly owner was subdued: times were tough and getting tougher; the remaining retailers in the area couldn't see much light at the end of the tunnel. What had changed? In a word, the casino.

The casino acted like a giant vacuum cleaner, said the shop owner, sucking in people with money to spend. As a result, people had largely abandoned the traditional shopping and dining neighbourhoods, which were now in danger of becoming ghost towns. Behind the image of glitter and pizazz and the catch-cry of 'let the good times roll' was a grim reality of struggle in the old neighbourhoods.

Mark had flown to Melbourne with his mind virtually made up. It was just a matter of giving himself extra reassurance by seeing the casino industry up close. But instead of leaving Melbourne with all lingering doubts resolved and convinced that his initial instincts were correct, he was uneasy. This issue was a lot less clear-cut than it appeared.

The deal

Back in Wellington, Mark reviewed the whole issue, going back over the casino plans and the economic-impact reports which had seemed to make an irresistible case.

The proposed casino would be a major development—but it would be a windowless building on a prime piece of waterfront land. Casinos didn't have windows, or clocks for that matter, because the operators wanted to create an environment in which gamblers lost track of time. Mark wondered if such a building would really fit in with the friendly and accessible waterfront he and the city council had been working to develop.

There was absolutely no doubt that the proposed casino would create jobs and bring in money, but what effect would it have on the shops in the retail precincts that the city had been promoting and investing in for the previous three years?

If people were drawn to the casino, what impact would that have on the flourishing café culture that had been so carefully nurtured?

Wellington had a busy theatre scene. Would live theatre and other such forms of entertainment be able to compete with the garish glamour and excitement of a casino?

Would tourists head straight for the casino? Would the

Wellington tourism experience be reduced to a session at the blackjack table or a couple of lost afternoons in front of a poker machine? Would visitors' abiding memory of the city be the inside of a windowless building, watching their money go down the drain in a blaze of artificial light?

Was that the vision of Wellington that had prompted Mark to run for mayor?

Mark wasn't against gambling. He'd enjoyed a flutter or two in his time, most of which had been small donations to the establishment. Having researched the subject thoroughly, he was confident that, with the proper support, the social costs of gambling could be contained and managed.

But what really worried him was the thought that the city might be giving away a prime waterfront site to an operation that would compromise and detract from — if not actually put in jeopardy — much of what the council had spent years working towards and building.

Looking at it from that point of view, he began to question whether a casino was really compatible with his and the council's vision for the city.

It would change the look and feel and vibe of a city that prided itself on being compact, friendly and easy to get around, and which offered a wide range of attractions and events, something for everyone.

The final cut

Decision day arrived. The final vote on the proposed casino dwarfed everything else on the agenda. That night it was the only game in town. There was a full turnout: all 15 councillors, including the mayor, were seated around the impressive U-shaped table in the Council Chambers. In front of each councillor a microphone protruded through the smooth leather table top. Beside each councillor was a stack of meeting papers. Some looked suspiciously unread.

Captured for posterity in expressions that suggested they took their responsibilities very seriously indeed, the previous mayors of Wellington looked down on proceedings. Whenever Mark glanced up at them, he couldn't help thinking of the old saying: 'He's no oil painting.' The public gallery was packed to overflowing and on the crammed media benches journalists jostled for space to set up their laptops. The scene was set.

Predictably, the debate pitted the undeniable economic benefits against the understandable social concerns. Sitting in the mayoral chair, Mark reflected that their counterparts in Melbourne must have hashed and rehashed the same arguments *en route* to making their decision.

The debate ebbed and flowed across the chamber. Passionate speeches were made for and against. It was always going to be close and as Mark discreetly did the numbers, the arithmetic was clear: it was all tied up. Everything now rested on his decision. The casino would stand or fall on his casting vote.

This fact ensured that he had the audience's full attention from the moment he opened his mouth. All eyes were on him. He began by thanking the councillors: they had considered the issues carefully under intense scrutiny from lobbyists and the media, and both sides had marshalled their arguments with intelligence and integrity to produce one of the finest debates he'd heard in the chamber.

However, in the weeks leading up to the debate, he'd come to realise that both sides were overlooking the key

point. It wasn't about whether casinos were good or bad *per se*. What it came down to was this: did a casino fit with their shared vision for the city, the vision that the public had so clearly endorsed at the recent election?

He related his experiences in Melbourne, describing the excitement and boom-town spirit surrounding the casino and the evidence that its success was coming at the expense of other parts of the city. He'd come to the conclusion that to give the casino the go-ahead would set in motion a chain of events leading to the elimination of the city's points of difference that everyone around the table had been working so hard to establish.

As it became clear that he was going to vote against the proposed casino, a murmur of surprise ran around the council table and through the galleries. In the hubbub some onlookers missed his concluding sentence: 'The city would have lost its slippers.'

Even those who picked up the cryptic comment assumed that they must have misheard him, because there'd been no mention of slippers in the debate. Besides, what on earth did slippers have to do with a casino? If you doubt that, just try getting into a casino wearing a pair.

When order was restored, Mark formally cast his vote against the application to build a casino in Wellington.

That made it official — it had been a close-run thing but Wellington would not be getting a casino.

For months afterwards, theories and rumours circulated as people tried to nail down the 'real' reason for the mayor's apparent change of heart which had, incidentally, surprised and angered some of his supporters.

Mark was confident that he'd made the right call. The casino probably would have been a very good one, but the Melbourne example suggested that it would have undermined everything the city had been working towards. Making a vision a reality involves measuring every project, every development, every initiative against it. The casino did not pass that test; it was not compatible with the vision. It would not have contributed to the city the mayor and council had been working to develop.

Counting the chips

The casino vote signalled the end of the council meeting. The chamber emptied quickly. The press had deadlines to meet, the public had seen what they'd come to see and the councillors split into two groups. One went off to celebrate, the other to commiserate.

As Mark gathered up his papers and prepared to go back to his office to shed the mayoral chains prior to heading home for what he felt would be a well-earned rest, he realised he wasn't alone. He glanced up to meet the steely gaze of Rachel, the manager of the gym he frequented. He hadn't noticed her in the public gallery, but seeing her now reminded him that she'd taken a close interest in the long-running casino debate, often buttonholing him on the subject while he was cycling or plodding away on the running machine. She'd left the mayor in absolutely no doubt that she was an enthusiastic supporter of the casino proposal. And while these conversations were rather one-sided as Mark saved his breath for his workout, he'd never expressed much disagreement as Rachel ticked off, yet again, all the reasons why the casino would be a boon for the city.

'Hi Rachel,' he said.

His smile wasn't returned. 'I can't believe you did that,' she snapped, then turned on her heel and headed for the door. After a few steps, she stopped and threw him another frosty glance over her shoulder. 'And I particularly can't believe that you could be so flippant about such an important decision. Just what the hell do slippers have to do with anything?'

Mark opened his mouth to reply but, before he could get a word out, Rachel was through the door and gone. His next visit to the gym promised to be an interesting one.

A tough workout

Mark had been going to the same gym for eight years. It wasn't one of those look-at-me places where the beautiful people gather to flaunt their toned and sculpted torsos, and certainly not a muscle factory frequented by hardcore body builders. It was a small but well-equipped gym located in a central city hotel; he'd gone there in the first place because it offered a corporate rate to his wife's law firm.

He stayed for four reasons. First, it has a couple of TV sets so he can watch sport as he works out. Second, it has a sauna and the staff ensure that there's always eucalyptus oil in the water which, in Mark's view, enhances the sauna experience twenty-fold. Third, it's not too busy, so not many people get to see what he looks like during a workout. Let's just say it's not a pretty sight. Fourth, since Rachel became the manager the gym has acquired a personal touch that he appreciates. The eucalyptus oil in the sauna was one of

Rachel's innovations. She'll bring clients a glass of water if they're pouring sweat as they pound away on the treadmill. She knows her clients' names, takes an interest in their professional activities and always has time for a chat. And not just an exchange of pleasantries, as Mark is well aware from their frequent conversations about the casino.

His routine is twenty minutes on the cross trainer, twenty minutes of stretches and weights, the same time on the bike or running machine (even though he hates running with a passion), and a five-minute wind-down. He's become pretty disciplined, so even though the day of the casino vote had left him drained, he was at the gym bright and early the next morning.

Rachel's greeting wasn't quite as fulsome as usual, which made him think she might keep her distance rather than challenge him over his decision to kill the casino. But when he saw her heading his way soon after he'd started on the cross trainer, he knew that had been a foolish thought. It just wasn't Rachel's style.

She didn't beat around the bush. Why had he voted against the proposal when everyone had expected him to support it? Plenty of other cities had casinos which seemed to be working fine — attracting tourism, stimulating business activity and creating jobs. With his casting vote Mark had gifted those other cities a permanent and significant edge over Wellington. And as for those bloody slippers, well, she was really looking forward to his explanation for that remark.

Mark took an even deeper breath. 'I'm glad you asked,' he said. He acknowledged that the slippers comment must have seemed odd and out of context, but it wasn't a throwaway line. In fact, the story behind it was quite central to his business career and, later, his decision to seek the mayoralty. And, yes, it had played a big part in changing his thinking on the casino proposal. It was a long story but if she was prepared to shout him a fruit juice after his workout, he'd spill the beans, slippers and all.

Perhaps thinking she'd just been conned out of a fruit juice, Rachel gave him a wary, somewhat sceptical nod: he had a deal.

The most unlikely source

Showered, changed and with a free juice in his hand, Mark settled into an armchair in the gym's foyer and proceeded to tell Rachel about the plumber who changed his life.

The best advice he'd received during his business career, he said, didn't come from one of those thick, forbidding business textbooks stuffed with technical data and abstruse theory. It wasn't delivered by a sleek management consultant with an MBA from Harvard, or a hard-driving CEO of a big company or major government agency, or even a mentor from among his many friends and contacts in the business community.

The biggest influence on his business career was a conversation with a plumber whom Mark had never met before and never saw again.

The time was 1989. The place was a newly opened Hannahs shoe store in Auckland. This was to be the company's flagship store, so a great deal was riding on it in terms of investment and the prestige of the Hannahs brand. A successful opening was essential.

As Hannahs national sales manager, Mark had been dispatched to Auckland to support the store manager and assist with staff training.

Whenever a new store opens, an advanced version of Murphy's Law kicks in: whatever can go wrong will go wrong, just at the moment you can least afford it. On the face of it, the opening was going well: the shop was busy but operating efficiently. Shoes were flying out the door.

Out the back, however, it was a different picture. A pipe in the bathroom had sprung a leak; the leak was threatening to become a flood and the first thing in its path would be the stock room. Mark was booked on a flight back to Wellington, but decided to stick around to make sure the problem was fixed. It proved an inspired decision.

To Mark's pleasant surprise, Murphy's Law seemed to have been suspended. The plumber had appreciated the urgency of the situation. He'd come straight in, fixed the leak quickly and with a minimum of fuss, and was now tidying up. The clean-up was as efficient as the repair: it was hard to tell there'd even been a leak or that a tradesman had been stomping around the premises.

As he paid the plumber at the back of the shop, Mark took the opportunity to thank him for a job well done and discovered that Peter wasn't your average plumber — he actually owned the company. More impressed by the minute, Mark offered him a fifty per cent discount on a pair of shoes, redeemable at any time.

Peter, it turned out, wasn't one to look a gift horse in the mouth, nor was he the sort of bloke who put off till tomorrow what he could do today. He needed a new pair of shoes, he had a bit of time up his sleeve, so he went straight out to the shop and selected a few pairs to try on. To make conversation as Peter was trying them on for size, Mark trotted out the old casual enquiry: 'So how's business?'

'Never been better'

'Well, actually,' said Peter, 'business is pretty good. Never been better, in fact.'

It takes quite a bit to send Mark's eyebrows skyward but that did the trick. This was 1989: most businesses had taken a serious hit in the wake of the 1987 stock market crash and were struggling just to keep their heads above water. In that tough economic environment he was used to people grumbling about how hard it was to make a buck. Hannahs, a well-established business, was doing all right but certainly not selling as many shoes as they would have liked.

'Good for you,' said Mark.

'Yeah,' said Peter reflectively. 'A year ago, I was just one of the crew at a big plumbing company. You know — clock in, do an honest day's work, clock out, pick up a cheque at the end of the week. I'd been there for years and, to be honest, I thought I'd finish up there. They were a pretty good outfit to work for — always plenty of work coming through the door and they paid reasonably well.' He shook his head and chuckled. 'Now I've got my own company with six blokes working for me.'

Mark made a mental note to bring out some more expensive shoes for Peter to try. Clearly a $200 pair of shoes was well within his price range. The conversation was also reinforcing Mark's conviction that you acquire more useful information talking with a customer rather than talking at him or her.

Mark was intrigued by Peter the Plumber's laconic tale. What was the secret of his success? How had he gone from being on someone else's payroll to employing six staff in what was obviously a thriving business? Most intriguing of all: how had he made such a shift and achieved such success in such a short time and in such a tough business environment?

As anyone who knows Mark Blumsky will attest, he'll never die wondering. Some people might have kept these questions to themselves. Not Mark: he said exactly what was on his mind. The answers he received would change the way he thought about business.

The most important business conversation

Mark: So Peter, what's your secret? How come you're doing so well when so many people are struggling? Believe me, I hear it all the time from customers and business contacts. People are doing it tough right now.

Peter: Well, when I was working for the other outfit, I came to realise just what an anonymous industry we really are. Most people couldn't tell you who their plumber is. They couldn't put a name to the last plumber they used. They might've written his name and number down somewhere, but rather than spend half an hour looking for it, they'll go to the Yellow Pages and just pick a name. I mean, can you remember the name of the last plumber you used?

Mark: I wouldn't have a clue. Like you said, I just look in the phone book and call the one with the biggest, most elaborate advert on the basis that if they can afford it, they must be doing something right.

Peter: It's strange: we remember all sorts of people's names. When we find a good service provider we make a point of going back to them time after time — but not plumbers. Hardly anyone remembers their plumber's name and they're quite happy to get any old one, even if the last guy did a really good job. Why should plumbers be different? I decided I had to change that and I think I've been reasonably successful.

Mark: Successful in making people remember you?

Peter: Absolutely. When people need a plumber, I want them to think of my company straight away.

Mark: So how did you go about it?

Peter: Well Mark, there are three things that we always take to a job. That's what my business is based on. These three things are, as you put it, the secret of my success. Now, you seem like a pretty switched-on guy: see if you can figure out what those three things are.

Mark: I bet one of them's a smile.

Peter: Nice try. Service with a smile is still a good principle but that's not one of them.

Mark: A positive attitude?

Peter: Nope. It's important, sure, but we don't have it to ourselves.

Mark: A sunny disposition?

Peter: That's just a smile combined with a positive attitude. No, you're on the wrong track, mate. You're thinking like one of those management gurus and coming up with stuff that applies to every walk of life. We're plumbers, remember. These are three things that help us do our job better.

Mark: A flash business card?

Peter: Mate, you're getting cold.

Mark: Fresh flowers as a thank-you for using your company?

Peter: Yeah, right. I can just imagine the reaction I'd get if I suggested that to the troops — short but not sweet, two words the second of which would be 'off'. Come on, Mark, you've heard the jokes about tradesmen and housewives. Put yourself in the shoes of a husband who's just on his way out to work: the doorbell rings and there's a plumber standing there with a bunch of flowers. If we went round doing that, we'd need bloody flak jackets.

Mark: Point taken. What about fresh coffee and a muffin?

Peter: Jesus, you're going from bad to worse. You'd be useless at Twenty Questions.

Mark: High-waisted pants?

Peter: Very funny. We're plumbers, mate, not builders. Most of us wear overalls.

Mark: And very grateful we are too.

Peter: Listen, put yourself in the customer's shoes: you answer the door and what do you see?

Mark: Okay, I open the door and there's a plumber standing there in his overalls, work boots, maybe a

	cap. And, of course, he's holding a bag of tools.
Peter:	Finally. Yes, mate, the first thing we take to a job is a bag of plumbing tools. How come you didn't think of that?
Mark:	I suppose I was trying to think of a gimmick that would make your company different, something a bit left field to make you really stand out from all the other plumbers.
Peter:	One sure way to stand out would be to turn up without tools. No tools, no plumbing.
Mark:	Okay, I give up. We'll be here all night otherwise. What's the second thing?
Peter:	This may be hard to believe but we always take a vacuum cleaner.
Mark:	Why didn't I think of that? It's so obvious: you're going out to unblock a drain, for God's sake don't forget the vacuum cleaner. You're kidding, right?
Peter:	I'm deadly serious. We take a vacuum cleaner so that we can clean up any mess we make.
Mark:	Why not just use the customer's vacuum cleaner?
Peter:	What if they don't have one? And even if they do have one, why should I clog up their vacuum cleaner with my mess? The point is, turning up with a vacuum cleaner tells the customer upfront:

Slippers: Service and Selling

'I might have to make a mess but I'm not going to walk away and leave you to clean it up. I'm going to fix your problem and leave your home as clean and tidy as I found it.' I want to send a very clear message about how I go about my business. Okay, you must be getting a feel for how I think about my work: any idea what the third thing is?

Mark: I'm not even going to try.

Peter: Go back to the plumber at the front door. What did I say he'd be wearing?

Mark: Overalls.

Peter: Right. Have you ever seen a clean pair of overalls?

Mark: No. I suspect the only time overalls are really clean is when they're put on for the first time.

Peter: You're not wrong. And what's he got on his feet?

Mark: Work boots.

Peter: Same question: have you ever seen a clean pair of work boots?

Mark: Same answer: not after day one.

Peter: Exactly. When we work outside, we tend to get a lot of crap on our boots. That's why the third thing we always carry is . . . a pair of slippers.

Mark: Excuse me?

Peter: A pair of slippers. Before we go into a customer's house, we take off our boots and put on a pair of slippers.

Mark: How do your guys feel about that?

Peter: It's not like we wear pink fluffy bunny slippers. It might look a bit funny, some hulking great bloke carrying a bag of tools and wearing slippers, but when we explain that we're taking off our dirty boots so we don't track mud though their house, people get it — and appreciate it. The slippers are actually the most important of the three things because they send a message that we think about our customers, that we recognise they've invited

us into their homes and that we care about the impression we leave.

Mark: Does it work?

Peter: We're flat out.

Mark: You must have good advertising.

Peter: We don't have any bloody advertising. Never have. It's all word of mouth. Everyone remembers the plumbers who put on their slippers before they come inside. They tell their friends about the slippers. We've got more work than we can handle. I'm actually thinking of taking on more staff because I'm turning away work.

Mark: More staff would mean more slippers.

Peter: Obviously.

Mark: Well, you've come to the right place.

The conversation that wouldn't go away

Mark never did sell Peter any slippers, but the conversation stayed with him. In fact, he couldn't get it out of his head.

There were moments when he decided Peter the Plumber's formula was actually a bit ridiculous: you ask for someone to come and fix a dripping tap but what you get is Mrs Doubtfire — a burly bloke in a pair of slippers with a vacuum cleaner under his arm.

But the more he thought about it, the more it made sense. He began to realise that the key to Peter's approach had nothing to do with plumbing; it was all about an attitude of caring for the customer. That was the point of difference distinguishing his operation from every other plumbing outfit in town.

And it was working — brilliantly. The simple fact was that, in a difficult economic environment, Peter was thriving while plenty of others were struggling.

This train of thought led him to the conclusion that Peter was actually an exceptional businessman. Peter wouldn't have called himself that; he probably didn't even think of himself as a businessman. The way he probably looked at it, he was just a plumber trying to carve out a little niche for himself and keep his customers happy.

He was doing business differently. He was taking a whole new approach that wasn't based on the fundamentals of his trade and, in the process, he was finding a way around the plumber's perennial marketing problems: how do I differentiate myself from every other plumber in the Yellow Pages? How do I create customer loyalty and generate repeat business?

One thing in particular that gnawed away at Mark was the fact that whenever he'd thought about plumbing — which wasn't often — he'd categorised it as humdrum, uninteresting, almost a necessary evil. A boring, dirty job but someone had to do it. Peter had created a point of difference that wasn't connected to the plumbing industry, which begged the question: could the principle be applied in other fields? The shoe business, for instance? Could Hannahs be different from all the other shoe companies? If so, how?

What the plumber taught the shoe salesman

Three things stood out:

- Peter the Plumber had a clear idea of what he wanted to do and where he wanted his business to go. He wanted his company to be remembered. In other words, he had a vision. Everything he did was designed to help make his vision a reality. Peter understood that just doing a good job didn't in itself contribute to that process: doing a good job was what most other plumbers did, it was what customers expected and it was certainly what they paid for. In order to stand out, he had to do something different and do it well.

- The key to Peter's success was that he had clear points of difference which instantly set him apart from every other plumber — the slippers and the vacuum cleaner. That was why people remembered his company.
- The slippers and vacuum cleaner weren't just gimmicks; they served a practical purpose. But they also served a larger purpose: they were symbols of Peter's attitude. He thought about his customers and cared about their property. In effect, he and his staff were putting themselves in the customer's shoes and doing what they'd appreciate from a tradesman working in their house. The slippers and vacuum cleaner sent his customers a simple, strong and welcome message: he cared. That was why they remembered Peter and his company.

It was working very well. If anything, Mark had underplayed his indifference to plumbers when answering Peter's question. Over the years he'd used dozens in various stores and at home but not a single name or face lingered in the memory. And he'd certainly never recommended a plumber to his friends. Until now.

Another glass of juice

Rachel was gobsmacked. That wasn't what she'd expected to hear at all. But while she was pleased that Peter the Plumber's innovative approach had worked for him, that didn't get Mark off the hook: in what way exactly, she asked, did the plumber's slippers justify Mark vetoing the casino?

'If we had a casino,' replied Mark, 'would you go to it?'

'You bet. Why do you think I wanted you to vote for it?'

'So, on Friday nights what would you do: go to that bar you like in Courtenay Place or go to the casino?'

'The casino, for sure.'

'That's the point. If everyone who'd normally go to Courtenay Place goes to the casino, what happens to Courtenay Place? Lots of other cities have casinos; Courtenay Place is our point of difference, our slippers.'

Rachel was silent for a few moments. 'Well, I can see

you're a true believer,' she said, 'so slippers obviously worked for Hannahs too?'

The short answer was 'no'. And if she shouted him another juice, he'd explain why not.

Time for a reality check

The slightly longer answer was that Hannahs didn't quite get it.

Mark had the sense that once Peter had done the hard work of establishing his three concepts — vision, point of difference and attitude — they were relatively easy to put into practice.

Could they work for Hannahs? Hannahs was one of the largest and most successful shoe store chains in the country, but increased competition and the fall-off in consumer spending had started to bite. Retail generally had become a whole lot tougher than it used to be. Mark believed he could nudge the company into doing things a bit differently — a bit more like Peter — and was convinced that would have a real impact on turnover.

Mark had been working for Hannahs since he was

thirteen, beginning as a parcel boy coming in after school and later joining full time after a short stint at university. Through the simple but effective device of selling lots of shoes, he rose through the ranks. The first step up was being made manager of the smallest store in a 100-strong chain at the age of nineteen. Fast-forward a decade and he was the national sales manager.

The job involved travelling around the country visiting stores in order to meet and motivate the 1000 or so staff. He was happy with his lot and his lifestyle: he met a lot of interesting people, he was well paid, he had a red sports car and a company credit card. What more could a young man want?

Not as simple as it seemed

The encounter with Peter had inspired Mark to try to do something similar in the footwear business. How hard could it be? After all, it was simple and successful. Who in their right mind wouldn't be all for it?

The problem was that the senior managers at Hannahs didn't share Mark's new-found enthusiasm for a point of difference or share his vision. They didn't accept the slippers story. If it ain't broke, don't fix it: they were perfectly happy doing what they'd always done; they reckoned they were doing a good job and the company was trucking along reasonably well. They couldn't see the sense, as they saw it, in changing a proven, successful formula for no good reason. In their eyes it was change for change's sake and that was a risky proposition.

Mark saw it very differently. Travelling around the country had brought home to him that footwear retail was boring and business was flat. The various shoe chains were selling pretty much the same products from shops you couldn't tell apart. Seen one shoe shop, you'd seen them all. The staff joked that the only differences between the rival chains was the sign above the door and the labels on the shoe box.

Sadly, that wasn't much of an exaggeration. Most senior people in the sector didn't seem to think there was any need to do anything differently or to stand out, which meant there was no pressure on people to innovate or be creative. It was a comfortable environment because you just had to keep doing the same old things.

Hannahs was a good company and had been a great employer, but since meeting Peter, Mark was starting to find it too comfortable and stuck in its ways. Where was the challenge? There had to be a better way of doing things but no one seemed very interested in finding it.

 A new business

Mark's inability to change Hannahs' entrenched culture didn't reduce his conviction that there was a better way for the shoe business. He still wanted to do for selling shoes what Peter had done for plumbing. He knew that opportunity still existed.

Over the years, Mark had come to realise that most people didn't consider shopping for shoes a fun thing to do. That couldn't all be blamed on the character of the hapless Al Bundy in the popular US sitcom *Married With Children*.

Most people regarded it as a chore, something to be endured rather than enjoyed. Many men were uncomfortable about taking off their shoes, perhaps because they had holes in their socks or were worried that their feet might smell. Some put themselves through all sorts of contortions to avoid revealing the holes in their socks. It was hard to know why they bothered because it never worked.

With kids it was more straightforward: the fact that they had to be dragged kicking and screaming into the shops made it pretty obvious that getting new shoes was among their least favourite activities.

The consensus seemed to be that shoe shopping was a pain in the backside, something you did as infrequently as possible and then, when the evil day couldn't be postponed, as quickly as possible. You didn't want to be in a shoe shop for a minute longer than was absolutely necessary.

Mark knew it didn't have to be like that. There had to be a way to make shoe shopping fun, maybe even an experience you looked forward to.

Nine months after Mark met Peter, he resigned from Hannahs to set up his own shoe business.

Making Mischief

Rachel was doubly gobsmacked. She found it very hard to believe that after working so hard to build a career with Hannahs and having such bright prospects, Mark could have turned his back on the company on the basis of a thirty-minute conversation with a plumber. And to walk away from that security to set up a business based on a pair of slippers didn't seem bold; it seemed downright crazy.

Mark had to agree that, when it was put like that, it did seem one hell of a gamble. At the time, though, it seemed the obvious, in fact the only, way to go. That was how deeply the conversation with Peter had affected him.

'I couldn't do that,' said Rachel. 'Leave a well-paid job with a great career path to do something with no guarantee of success. That's way too scary.'

Mark reminded her that she'd actually done something similar: despite not having any management experience, she'd given up a safe job as an instructor at one of the city's biggest and most successful gyms to become the manager of a much smaller, lesser-known establishment with a completely different client base.

'I took the gamble,' he said, 'because I believed there was the opportunity to set up a shoe business using the same principles that Peter's plumbing business was based on. The attraction was that my company wouldn't be restricted or confined by any rules or preconceptions about how you had to operate. I could do what I liked. I didn't care about the conventional wisdom of how a shoe shop should look or operate because I was committed to doing things differently. The challenge was to find our slippers and then figure out how to present them to the customers.'

The obvious starting point was the shop's name. The name would set the tone and send out a clear message, letting customers know before they'd even set foot in the place that this wasn't your average shoe shop. Mark wanted people to know just by looking at the sign above the door that if they stepped inside, they were going to have a different sort of shoe-shopping experience.

Casting an eye over the industry, it was plain to see that if Mark could come up with a striking, interesting, intriguing or otherwise different name, he'd have an immediate point of difference because virtually all shoe stores had completely boring names. The names fell into three categories:

- Founder: 'Neville's Shoes'
- Location: 'Main Street Shoes'
- Price: 'Value Shoes'

Well, 'Mark's Shoes' was no better than 'Neville's Shoes' and a cut-price operation wasn't what he had in mind. 'Main Street Shoes' was fine if the customer was lost but otherwise had nothing to recommend it.

Mark's vision was to make shoe shopping fun. He wanted people to enjoy being in his shoe store. He wanted to change the industry. It seemed obvious that a fun store should have a fun name.

His friends were full of ideas such as 'Happy Feet' or 'You Shoes, You Lose'. Unfortunately, none of their self-styled brilliant suggestions hit the mark. In desperation, he hunted through dictionaries and a thesaurus for words that conveyed the idea of fun. He found 'mischief'.

It was perfect. Mischief is a fun word. It's a word that actually makes people smile when they hear it or read it or say it. They can't help themselves.

A different kind of store

Now he had a name. That wasn't so hard. The next step was developing the completely different shopping experience. The idea was to turn shoe shopping on its head: what had previously been a chore would become enjoyable. People might come into the store looking like they were about to bury a beloved pet but they'd walk out with a smile.

Once he'd fixed on the premise that his store had to look and feel different from every other shoe shop, the ideas began to flow.

The staff would wear brightly coloured shirts in a variety of styles rather than boring old black and grey uniforms. The colours would change from day to day — 'If the Mischief crew are wearing purple, it must be Friday.' The shirts would be so popular with the staff that they'd often wear them when they went out on the town, and when a group of them were out together people would think they were a band or a troupe of acrobats. The last thing they'd think would be, 'Oh, those guys obviously work in a shoe shop.'

The store would be well-lit and painted in cheerful colours. The atmosphere would be a world away from the dim, dark, leathery, soulless, uninviting places that most shoe shops were.

The shoe boxes would be stacked out the back in the storeroom rather than scattered round the store for customers to trip over and creating an impression of mess and disorganisation.

Mischief would not try to be all things to all men and women. It would not sell all varieties of shoe to all ages. Mischief would cater to people aged between eighteen and forty-five.

There would be a message board outside the shop. Every day, Mark would write a new message designed to make people stop, read, think, smile or shrug. (Back in the dark ages before the internet, coming up with a new message every day would prove a lot harder than he'd expected. He ended up getting most of his ideas from the radio show he listened to in the shower.)

There would be a water cooler in the corner so customers could be offered a glass of cold water. On hot days they wouldn't wait to be asked; they'd help themselves. On really hot days they'd form a queue.

Everyone who came into the shop would be offered a lollipop. The lollipop bowl would appear as soon as they entered the shop because it would be a reward for coming in, not for spending their money.

Children would be given a Mischief balloon. Big kids would get one too if they asked nicely.

Even the Mischief carry bags would be different: bright pink with strong handles to encourage re-use. People would carry their lunch or their gym gear in them. They'd be seen everywhere — instant branding.

When things were a bit quiet, Mark would get a couple of part-timers to walk round town with their bright pink Mischief bags filled with shoe boxes. People would notice and wonder what was going on at this new place. In fact, they'd assume that something exciting must be happening at Mischief. Why else would they be seeing so many of those pink bags around town? Occasionally, for his private amusement, Mark would get the part-timers to stroll past rival shoe shops, happily swinging their pink bags, and then wait and see how long it would be before someone from that shop wandered past Mischief trying to look casual as they sought to get a handle on the promotion that was generating all these sales. It wouldn't take long.

He'd play upbeat music in the shop, rather than the elevator muzak you heard everywhere else. It would lift the mood and if the staff occasionally broke into a boogie, that would be fine by him. In fact, every so often they might whisk a lucky customer out of their seat for a free dance lesson.

Mischief would be the first store in the country with a foot massage machine. It would come all the way from Germany and have hundreds of tiny rubber nipples on a vibrating flat mat surface and have the same effect as a gentle tickle. The free foot massages would be hugely popular.

The staff would be encouraged to engage in a little Mischief making every now and again. The machine had a turbo setting which sent it into overdrive and, occasionally, just as a customer was really getting into their soothing foot massage, the staff member operating the machine would surreptitiously alert the other staff who'd gather round to watch the fun when the turbo switch was accidentally on purpose flicked, increasing the speed twenty-fold. Most customers would see the funny side of it and join in the hilarity. When they'd stopped squealing, that is. By then they would have figured out that the store was called Mischief for a reason.

He would establish all these points of difference, the big and the little, to make Mischief completely different from the competition and ensure that customers would never forget shopping there.

A different kind of service – Ten out of Ten

Ensuring that Mischief Shoes looked different to every other shoe shop in town was important, but it wasn't enough. The physical, visual differences in the store had to be backed up by a staff attitude that reflected and advanced the vision of having fun.

To that end Mark introduced a range of new customer-service techniques and strove to create a new, positive attitude. This was the final piece in the slippers jigsaw.

The key component in establishing this new attitude was the Ten out of Ten initiative.

Ten out of Ten consisted of ten actions or techniques that Mark wanted to see employed in every interaction with a potential customer. Derived from his experience and research, they were a combination of pointers, must dos and service techniques. If a staff member delivered all ten, it was odds on that the customer would be blown away by the quality of their shopping experience.

Whenever a staff member had finished with a customer, Mark would ask, 'Did you get ten out of ten?'

The Top Ten

1. Say 'Hi', 'How are you ?', 'Great to see you' or some other cheery greeting — as opposed to 'Can I help you?'
2. Offer them a seat, make them comfortable, take their shoes off.
3. Offer a glass of water, particularly on a hot day.
4. Offer a lollipop — everyone likes something free.
5. Get a staff member to clean the customer's old shoes while they're trying on new ones — and make sure the customer notices.
6. Bring the customer more than one pair of shoes to try on. Be prepared to offer choices and take the time to get it right. Surprise them by demonstrating that you really want to help them to find the right shoes — as opposed to wanting to get rid of them ASAP.
7. Put the new shoes on for the customer or at least offer to do so.
8. Tell them what the new shoes are made of and where they come from.
9. Explain how best to clean the new shoes, thus

demonstrating that you want them to get value from their purchase.
10. Mention the loyalty club when you say goodbye.

The aim was to get ten out of ten every time. The staff bought into the concept and Ten out of Ten became an integral component of the Mischief culture.

Crucially, not one of the ten techniques actually related to selling shoes. The customer experience, rather than the sale, was the focus.

In fact, staff who'd made a sale, even a big-ticket one, could find themselves on the mat if their attitude was wrong and they scored poorly out of ten. In the long run a ten out of ten with no sale was better than a two out of ten with a sale because the customer who'd had a good experience was more likely both to come back to Mischief and to spread positive word-of-mouth messages. The customer who walked out with a new pair of shoes but without a positive feeling about Mischief was unlikely to do either.

It was all about creating a relationship with the customer. A Ten out of Ten pretty much guaranteed that.

Mark was aware that the conventional notion of an efficient retail operation consisted of a single-minded focus on sales and a real reluctance to 'waste time' on browsers or even discretionary shoppers. These were the people who might buy a pair of shoes if something caught their eye, as opposed to 'need' shoppers — those who'd come in because they needed a new pair of shoes today. But that attitude was contrary to his philosophy of the shopping experience.

The Ten out of Ten concept can apply to any role within any form of business. It's about identifying ten little things a person can do to make a good impression. It's as relevant to a law practice as a call centre. The key rule is that the actual outcome — making a sale, dealing with a complaint, compiling a report — can't be on the list.

Exceeding expectations

It's all about exceeding people's expectations. People come into a shoe shop expecting to buy a pair of shoes. They expect basic service: someone to show them the shoes and take their money. They don't expect to be amazed or delighted by a lot of other things.

Since meeting the plumber, Mark was more focused on whether the suppliers and service providers he dealt with met, exceeded or failed to live up to his expectations. He had a problem with some lights in his apartment which had very high ceilings. He got out the ladder, set it up and climbed — right to the top. And when he got to the top, he decided that it really wasn't a very good idea so he climbed down and rang an electrician. The electrician came in, did a quick, efficient job and went on his way. An hour later Mark had forgotten his name and had only a vague recollection of what he looked like.

Remembering the plumber, Mark asked himself: how could that electrician have left an impression on me? He could have given me a pack of candles and a lighter, saying, 'Thanks for your business and if your power ever gets shut off, use these candles to light up your life.' And when Mark looked closer, he'd notice the little sticker on the candles with the electrician's name and phone number. That would be the first thing he saw when he lit the candles.

But the electrician didn't even leave a business card, which was the least Mark expected him to do.

In marked contrast was the ex-Hannahs clerk who stopped Mark in the street one day to say he was now working for himself cleaning cars. He gave Mark his card; Mark said all the right things, promised to give him a call next time his car needed a clean, and promptly forgot about it. The car cleaner didn't. A little later he rang Mark to put him on the spot:

you said you might want your car cleaned about now. Mark thought 'good for you' and gave him the business.

It cost $100 and for a split second Mark thought, 'Okay, well you got me that time but you won't do it again.' Then he noticed that not only had the guy made a very good job of cleaning the car, he'd blackened the wheels. And when he got in the car, he saw that not only was the interior immaculate but the guy had attached a nice air freshener to the air-conditioning system.

There was a CD in the CD player — *Frank Sinatra's Greatest Hits* — and beside the CD case on the passenger seat was a note saying, 'I just thought you might enjoy listening to Ol' Blue Eyes on your next drive.'

The car cleaner had exceeded expectations. Far from feeling ripped off, Mark wrote out the cheque with the satisfied air of a customer who has got value for money.

Why can't I help you?

'Can I help you?' was banned in Mischief.

Some of the staff were initially puzzled by this. After all, it's a phrase you hear all the time. Practically every salesperson in just about every shop in every city in the English-speaking world trots it out on a regular basis. Was it really that bad?

Mark thought so. He knew from years of experience and observation that there was something about the phrase that put people off, to the extent that people who really needed help were inclined to say, 'No thanks. Just looking.' It was even more off-putting when it was yelled from the other side of the shop or from behind the shop counter, as was often the case.

First impressions were important, if not vital. 'Can I help you?' tended to sound automatic, uninterested, insincere, almost dismissive, as if the speaker can't quite understand why the other person was on the premises. Rather than create an impression of warmth and welcome in those critical first few moments, it was more likely to throw up a barrier. In many ways, welcoming people into your shop should be no different than welcoming them into your home. You should be pleased to see them. You should be happy to show them around and make them feel comfortable and relaxed.

A friendlier, less stitched-up approach seemed to put people at ease and encourage them to engage with staff and ask for advice. It also encouraged the staff to be more creative and less repetitive: they actually had to think about what they were going to say. It brought their personalities into play right from the word go:

- G'day! How's your day going? I hope you're enjoying being out and about and doing some shopping this afternoon.
- Thanks for coming into Mischief. Is there something in particular you're looking for?
- Going by the number of bags you're carrying, you're doing some serious shopping. Are new shoes on the list? Hope so! You can manage at least one more bag.
- Hi. Hope you're enjoying the chance to have a look around Mischief. Just make sure you don't get into too much mischief while you're here.

The Moment of Truth

Mark was a huge believer in the importance of first impressions. He hardly ever bothered to read CVs. They always made the person seem like God's gift to shoe retailing, but that was impossible — the role was already filled. Seriously, they tended to make the person sound too good to be true: Mark had never seen a CV that owned up to the most minor shortcoming.

He much preferred to meet people face to face. More often than not he would know within twenty seconds whether a person would be suitable for a particular sales role. When he was recruiting at Mischief, he was looking for a spark, a positive attitude, a bit of confidence, a hint of personality. If the person had those attributes, Mischief could do the rest by providing training and developing the requisite specific skills. Mark had the confidence to turn someone like that into a Mischief salesperson.

His recruitment method was based on the concept of The Moment of Truth: the defining moment in most customer-staff relationships. The impression created during the first twenty seconds of interaction was incredibly hard to undo. Did the customer like you, feel comfortable with you, want to talk to you? If the answer was yes, a relationship could be formed and trust established. If not, the opportunity had gone, probably never to return.

The Moment of Truth wasn't confined to Mark's first exposure to a job applicant or a staff member's first interaction with a customer. There were instances when members of the public had a moment of truth with the store itself.

Mischief had a policy of never barring entrance to someone who wanted to shop. If someone knocked on the door before the store had opened or after closing time, the staff would unlock the door and usher them in. Mark wanted those customers to remember Mischief as the shop that especially opened for them, rather than the one where the staff ignored them in the hope that they'd get the message and go away.

Just getting started

Seeing Mark glance at his watch, Rachel assumed he was signalling that he wanted to wrap the conversation up.

'Hey, I appreciate you taking the time to explain,' she said. 'I realise now there's more to slippers than meets the eye. Mischief must have been a fun place to work.'

'I'm just getting started,' said Mark. He was heartened that Rachel seemed to be getting the slippers message — vision, points of difference and attitude — especially given that she'd embarked on the conversation thinking he'd lost the plot. But he hadn't explained how he'd managed to introduce the concept to the council or answered the indignant question that had set off the discussion in the first place: why had he referred to slippers when outlining his reasons for voting against the casino?

'To be continued,' he said. 'Tomorrow the juice is on me.'

Round Two

At about two o'clock that afternoon Mark went out for a bite of lunch. He decided to try a new café he'd heard good things about. It certainly looked inviting from the street and the blackboard menu outside made his mouth water. The only trouble was he was a few minutes too late. 'We shut at two,' the manager told him without a hint of regret. Perusing the empty food cabinets, Mark wondered out loud what had happened to the filled rolls and sandwiches which must have been there at 1.59 pm — or had they completely sold out? They'd been packed up and put away, replied the manager.

The incident was still in Mark's mind as he chatted to Rachel the next morning. It reminded him of a famous story he'd heard, the moral of which was that a little extra service or effort could go a long way:

A hugely wealthy businessman — we'll call him Max the Multimillionaire — had been attending a conference in a pretty little country town. In other words, he and three of his mates had spent the day on the local golf course.

After lingering at the 19th hole, they got back into the centre of town quite late. There were only two places to eat but both were on the verge of closing for the night, literally in the process of hanging up the 'closed' sign in the window.

Bob and co went into the first restaurant and asked for a table for four. The owner thought about it, looked at his watch, and told them, sorry the place was closed. He made the choice to get home at what he obviously considered to be a reasonable hour rather than accept their business.

They went across the road where the staff were putting the chairs up on the tables.

Once again Bob asked for a table for four. Tom, the owner, hesitated. He gestured at the chairs on the tables and the just swept floor. He was sorry but they'd just closed for the night.

Bob asked Tom to reconsider. He and his mates had played 36 holes of golf that day and hadn't had anything to eat since a quick sandwich between rounds. They were absolutely starving. They weren't after a five-course meal, just something quick and easy to fill the gap.

Tom shrugged. Okay, he said, but the cook had already left so all he could offer was reheated soup and toasted sandwiches. Fine, said Bob.

A table was set up. Tom sent the rest of his staff home and prepared the food himself. It wasn't flash but it was hot and tasty and there was plenty of it and it went down a treat. The bill came to $30.

Bob pulled out his chequebook. He thanked Tom and announced he was going to leave a tip, but there was a condition attached: tomorrow Tom had to go across the road and show the owner of the other restaurant the cheque.

The following day Tom went over to the other restaurant and asked the owner if he remembered Bob and his mates. Yeah, was the reply: they'd turned up after closing time and expected him to re-open the kitchen just for their benefit. The manager shook his head, as if to say, 'Some people are unbelievable; they think the world revolves around them.'

Tom told him what had happened after that: how

Bob and friends had come to his place, which was also closed, but he'd relented and rustled up soup and toasted sandwiches.

The other owner shook his head again. 'Mate, you're a soft touch,' he said. 'You can't let people take advantage of you like that.'

'Oh well,' said Tom handing him the cheque. 'At least they tipped.'

Figuring the tip would be a pittance, the other owner glanced at the cheque. It was for $30,030.

Wedding shoes

Mark told Rachel that he'd taken that story to heart, which was why Mischief would always open its doors to anyone who wanted to shop. The policy paid dividends one Sunday morning when Mark was in doing some stocktaking. A clearly agitated young man in a full morning suit began banging on the door. Mark opened up and all was revealed:

'Mate, I know you're shut but I really need your help. I've just arrived in town and I'm getting married in an hour but the airline lost the bag which my black shoes are in. If

What the plumber taught the mayor about business

I turn up at the church in these trainers, my fiancée will probably call the whole thing off. And if she doesn't, her mother sure as hell will.'

A few minutes later, a far more relaxed groom-to-be strode out of the shop in a pair of smart black shoes carrying a pink Mischief bag containing his old trainers.

Just out of curiosity, Mark kept an eye on the marriage notices in the newspaper that week. Sure enough, there it was — along with a footnote thanking Mark at Mischief for his outstanding service and invaluable help in getting the groom to the altar in a respectable state.

Mark cut out the article and stuck it on the staffroom notice board. You can't buy that kind of advertising.

 Service never ends

Rachel couldn't understand how people could go into business without understanding and appreciating the importance of the customer. Why would you discourage potential customers? Why would you turn people away when all they wanted to do was spend their money in your establishment? Wasn't that the whole point of the exercise? Mark told her it happened all too often; in fact, it had happened to him yesterday. He assumed those who did it saw it as controlling their workload but they seemed oblivious to the long-term effects on their business.

Power of the positive

By now Rachel had got slippers between her teeth. She wanted to know if Mark had any other secrets for building up a new business. One big one came to mind: 'Don't be negative, always be positive.' Mark's whole attitude to life was to focus on the positive — his glass was always half full. In his experience the importance of being positive was widely underestimated in business. Rachel gave him a sceptical look. Wasn't all that glass half full, power of positive thinking stuff really just an empty slogan trotted out by the New Age touchy-feely brigade? She challenged Mark to spell out exactly how being positive could help in business.

'It puts you in the mindset to find solutions,' he said. 'Being negative steers you into that "we're stuffed so why bother?" attitude. Being positive is no guarantee of success, but it gives you a chance to achieve success; being negative gives you no chance. It's like buying a lottery ticket. Some people never buy one because they assume they'll never win. Well, the simple reality is that unless you buy a ticket, you can't possibly win. You're not giving yourself a chance.'

Shoes — lots of shoes

One of the Ten out of Ten principles was bringing out a range of shoes for a customer to try even if they were pretty clear about what they wanted. Part and parcel of that was not being negative. Mark had seen this exchange a hundred times:

Customer: 'Hello. I'd like to try on these shoes.'
Staff: 'Of course. What size do you take?'
Customer: 'I'm pretty sure I'm an eight.'
Staff: 'Sorry, we're out of eights. We've only got sevens and nines.'
Customer: 'Oh, well, that's a pity. Thanks anyway.'

At which point the customer leaves, probably never to return.

The staff member might have thought they were simply stating the inescapable fact that there were no size eights of that particular shoe in stock. They might even have expected a pat on the back for being on top of the stock situation. But neither the establishment nor the customer gets any benefit from that sort of rigid approach.

Mark trained his staff to handle that situation very differently. It often produced a very different result.

Customer: 'Hello. I'd like to try on these shoes please.'
Staff: 'Certainly. What size do you take?'
Customer: 'I'm pretty sure I'm an eight.'

Staff: 'Excellent. Have a seat and take off your shoes. Sally will get you a glass of water. Derek doesn't look busy so I'll get him to give your shoes a polish while I duck out the back and find a pair of eights.'
Customer: 'Thanks.'

At this point the staff member goes out to the storeroom hoping against hope that there's a pair of size eights hidden away in a corner. Of course there aren't. There are sevens and nines for Africa but no size eights. The situation is exactly the same but it's possible to achieve a better outcome.

There are two options at this point:

Option 1: Be upfront
Staff: 'Sorry, we don't have any size eights.'
Customer: 'Oh, well that's a pity. Thanks anyway.'

Once again, no sale, but at least the customer has got to sample the Mischief experience — friendly service, a drink of water, a lollipop and a free shoe shine. They've got a lot more out of their visit than if they'd simply been informed at the get-go that their size wasn't available. Still, it's still far from ideal because the customer didn't get what he or she was really there for.

Option 2: Offer alternatives

Staff: 'But the good news is that we do have these three similar styles of shoe in your size — if you've got the time to try them on.'

Customer: 'Seeing I'm here I might as well. Hey, these are quite nice . . .'

Staff: 'They are, aren't they? Stand up and have a walk around in them, see how they feel. They certainly look good — check them out in the mirror.'

Mark found that most customers were prepared to try the alternatives because they had a shoe-shopping mindset. They'd come into the shop to look at and maybe buy shoes and now they were being encouraged to try on a range.

The people who got this treatment in Mischief seemed to appreciate the staff going the extra mile on their behalf. Surprisingly few stuck fast to their original choice, either by asking if a pair of size eights could be ordered in or having no interest in considering the alternatives that had been picked out. This was because the alternatives were never dramatically different: if the shopper had picked out black brogues, you wouldn't offer him brown cowboy boots. And a surprising number would end up buying two pairs from the range of options presented to them.

While other stores would only ever bring out one pair, Mark believed that being offered a choice was a component of the positive experience. He didn't want his staff to assume they knew exactly what the customer wanted. Equally, he didn't want them to assume that the customer knew exactly what he or she wanted. Providing options helped sales and contributed to the store's positive reputation.

It's all in the way that you ask

Mark first observed the difference a positive attitude could make at a petrol station. As Hannahs New Zealand sales manager, he spent a lot of time on the road visiting the stores, which meant he stopped at a lot of petrol stations to fill up his red sports car.

What usually happened was that an attendant would wander over while he was at the pump and ask, 'Oil and water okay?' Mark would always say, 'Yep, fine thanks.'

In fact, Mark didn't have the faintest idea whether his oil and water were fine. For all he knew, the red sports car could have been running on empty. Deep down he suspected that one of these days he was going to find out the hard way that he really should have had both oil and water checked when he had the chance. Until that happened, though, he'd go on saying they were fine — like most people did.

The problem was 'Oil and water okay?' was the service station equivalent of 'Can I help you?' — an automatic query with an unmistakable implication of hoping that the offer wouldn't be taken up. And 'Yep, fine thanks' was the motorist's equivalent of 'No thanks, just looking'.

There had to be a better way to approach it. After all, it really was high time that someone who understood cars a lot better than he did had a look under the bonnet to ensure that the oil and water situation wasn't critical. The red sports car's health depended on it.

He got his wish in a one-pump service station way out in the country. The attendant came over and, rather than asking a half-hearted question, said firmly but politely, 'Could you open the hood so I can check your oil and water?'

Mark popped open the bonnet and the attendant started poking around. 'Your oil is a bit low,' he said, 'so I'll top it up for you.' Mark drove away feeling better about his car and grateful towards the attendant. The fact that he'd spent more than he'd intended didn't even cross his mind.

It was a matter of approaching the same situation in a different, more positive, more assertive manner to achieve a much better outcome for all concerned — the car, the car owner and the supplier.

That little service station must have had one of the best oil-to-petrol sales ratios in the country simply because they availed themselves of an opportunity and added value. No doubt they prolonged the life of a few cars too.

Every industry probably has a phrase that's holding back business. It might be used by many people with the best of intentions, but it can still have a negative impact.

The power of no

At Mischief Mark hammered the theme of always being positive because he'd seen what a negative answer could do, even when it was entirely accurate.

Once, on a plane, Mark got into conversation with the guy in the next seat; it turned out they were staying at the same hotel. This hotel had a great reputation and at first sight well and truly lived up to it: the lobby was spectacular, the flowers on display were beautiful, the two staff members at reception were immaculately groomed. Mark's check-in went smoothly but his new friend was not so lucky.

Slippers: Service and Selling

The conversation went something like this:

Guest: Hi, I have a reservation. The name's Milne.

Check-in: Sorry, sir, we don't seem to have a reservation under that name.

Guest: That can't be right — I booked a couple of weeks ago. Can you check?

Check-in: Okay, let's see . . . Oh, yes, here we are. Sorry about that. Now you are aware that the rooms don't become available till two o'clock?

Guest: No problem. I'll head into town on the courtesy coach and grab a bite of lunch. While I'm here, can I organise a late check-out for tomorrow?

Check-in: Sorry, sir, we have a conference starting here tomorrow. The participants have arranged early check-in so we'll need your room.

Guest: Oh, that's a bit of a problem. I see the courtesy coach is about to leave: can you hold it for a couple of minutes while we sort this out?

Check-in: No, sir, the coach operates on a strict schedule. It must leave on time.

Guest: Well, can you at least have my bags taken up to the room?

Check-in:	I'm afraid not, sir. Only the concierge can do that and he's driving the coach.
Guest:	Can I leave my bags with you, behind the reception desk?
Check-in:	No, that's against hotel policy. If you just want to leave them over there in the corner, the concierge will take care of them when he gets back.

As it turned out the coach ended up leaving late anyway, with a very disgruntled guest on board. Mr Milne gave the impression that, all things considered, he'd rather be in a war zone. His bags were eventually taken to a room — but not his room.

When he retold this story, Mark used to joke that he hadn't heard so many knock-backs since his dating days. For him, the point was that while the receptionist might have been absolutely correct on every count, she'd handled the encounter in a way that was practically guaranteed to ruin Mr Milne's day. He would not stay there again.

With a little creativity and a more positive attitude, it could have been a much pleasanter, more productive interaction:

- I'm just confirming your reservation, sir. I'm sure it's here — just bear with me.'

Slippers: Service and Selling

- 'We have a large conference group arriving tomorrow so there could be a bit of a problem with a late check-out, but we'll do our very best for you.'
- 'I'll ask the driver to wait a couple of minutes. If the coach isn't too full, it shouldn't be a problem.'
- 'Leave your bags where they are, sir. We'll find somewhere for them until the concierge returns.'

That approach doesn't necessarily give Mr Milne exactly what he wants either, but he wouldn't have spent the next five years running down the hotel and discouraging people from staying there. And if they'd really gone out of their way for him or done a little something to make up for what they couldn't do for him, Mr Milne would have remembered them for the right reason and would have been happy to tell others about his positive experience.

Handbags at ten paces

Mark experienced something similar at first hand during a shopping expedition in Auckland. Looking for a present for his wife, he noticed that one of the fashionable shops was running a mega-sale which included a line of handbags slashed to half-price. In among the display of half-priced handbags was one in particular that he knew his wife would love. He picked it out and carried it up to the counter feeling mighty pleased with himself.

The sales assistant couldn't find a price tag on it. Mark pointed out that all the handbags displayed in the sale section were the same reduced price, but the assistant said he needed the tag to complete the sale. When a search of the display area failed to locate the tag, he called the assistant manager. She wasn't prepared to let the sale go through without the tag either. After all, she said, this particular handbag mightn't have been in the sale: someone might have put it in the display by accident or Mark might have picked it up somewhere else.

Having offended the customer by implying that he might have done something dishonest, she said she'd have to get the floor manager to resolve the issue. Five minutes later, when the floor manager still hadn't appeared, Mark walked out of the shop. He was disappointed that his wife would miss out on a nice gift, but there's a limit to how many obstacles an eager customer should have to overcome.

Once again the staff thought they were doing the right thing by following the rules, but they could have handled the situation very differently. Imagine if the sales assistant had said:

> 'Yes, that is a lovely handbag. I see the tag's missing but I'm pretty sure it's in the sale, so I'll ring it up at the reduced price. Just to be on the safe side, though, I'll take down your details and confirm the price later. If I've overcharged you, I'll send you a refund; if I've undercharged you, well, this is your lucky day.'

That would have made Mark go 'Wow', which is exactly the reaction a business should want its customers to have. Chasing the wow factor involves trusting staff to make customer-service decisions which deliver a positive experience for the customer, rather than binding staff with a set of rules and regulations aimed at ensuring that every transaction is done by the book. The likelihood is that such a top-down approach won't impress either your customers or your staff.

Satisfied customers are often a business's best marketing tool. In this day and age of round-the-clock wall-to-wall advertising, a genuine, personal recommendation carries a lot of weight. The plumber who never had to advertise was well aware of the power of word of mouth.

What the plumber taught the mayor about business

Keeping it real

It bemused and amused staff from other shoe stores to see Mark sweeping the footpath in front of Mischief each morning before he opened for business. They used to joke that Mark should have read his job description more carefully. A couple of the other owners never got tired of wandering over to ask Mark whether he'd mind giving the footpath outside their shop a quick sweep while he was at it.

They obviously saw it as a bit demeaning and not the best use of his time and expertise. He begged to differ for three reasons:

1. Many customers, coming across him sweeping the footpath, would stop for a chat. In the course of these chats Mark learned a lot about his customer base, including the fact that they credited him with having a real pride in his shop.
2. It wasn't lost on the staff that the boss didn't mind getting his hands dirty and doing the least-fancied jobs. That made it easier for him to ask them when it was their turn to do the menial tasks and made it a lot harder for them to say no.

3. Pitching in, even with the menial tasks, gave Mark a good handle on how the store was actually functioning at all levels: he knew how long a given job should take to do and which jobs were more problematical than met the eye.

Mark firmly believed that the best way to get to know your business back to front was to work in it rather than to sit back and watch your employees work. That was why he swept the footpath and served customers. That was why, when he was mayor, he'd spend a day dishing out parking tickets or answering the phones. It helped him understand the business of running a city.

Not a typical Monday morning . . .

Most of the pedestrians hurrying to work in the central business district on a blustery Monday morning were too preoccupied to notice the mayor deep in conversation with a couple of city parking wardens.

The few who did notice couldn't resist having a joke at the mayor's expense. Some advised Mark to pay the fine and scram before a press photographer arrived; others advised the wardens not to let the mayor talk his way out of it.

Mark smiled and waved, happy to let them have their little jokes. His car hadn't left the garage that morning. Rather than having run foul of the parking wardens, he was actually on patrol with them, even to the point of writing out tickets.

It was a revealing experience. Among other things, he found himself on the receiving end of the abuse that parking wardens put up with on a daily basis from people who seemed to think they had a God-given right to park wherever they wanted, for however long they wanted.

Interestingly, some of the worst abuse came from the most — on the face of it, anyway — respectable people, the sort of people who, after a couple of glasses of pinot noir, can often be heard deploring the decline in standards of behaviour. An example was the impeccably dressed middle-aged man who looked for all the world like a bank manager or a senior partner in a law firm. Ticketed for illegally blocking a fire hydrant with his late-model European car, he responded with a foul-mouthed barrage, the sort of stuff you'd expect to hear from a young hoon reeling out of a bar at two in the morning. Mark couldn't believe his ears.

As mayor, he'd copped his share of angry feedback from

the disgruntled public: people who saw themselves as being adversely affected by a council decision were always quick to let him know. However, their tirades were generally delivered in writing, because most people find it easier to give someone a piece of their mind via a keyboard rather than in person.

For the parking wardens, though, face-to-face verbal abuse was pretty much part of the job. The worst part.

Mr Potty Mouth only had himself to blame. He hadn't reached middle age without being aware that if you flouted parking regulations, you ran the risk of getting a parking ticket. He'd gambled and lost. If he wasn't prepared to run the risk of a ticket, he could have driven a couple of hundred metres down the road and parked legally.

Going out with the parking wardens wasn't what you'd

call fun, but it was a useful exercise. The mayor's office received more complaints about parking tickets than all other council functions combined. It was useful for Mark to get a feel for the job, to see how people treated the wardens and to observe how often it was a case of the nastier the outburst, the shakier the grounds for complaint.

From that day on he looked at parking ticket complaints a little differently. If Mr Potty Mouth had written an indignant letter in an attempt to get off the ticket, you could bet your bottom dollar his version of events would have omitted his volley of swear words. Instead he would have cast himself as the innocent victim of conniving and malicious wardens.

....Nor a typical Monday afternoon

Mark spent the afternoon on the phone.

First, he recorded a voice message for the new council phone system so that when the switch board became overloaded, callers heard the following first message:

'Hi. Welcome to the Wellington City Council, this is Mayor Mark Blumsky speaking. Sorry, all our lines are a bit busy at the moment but we'll be with you soon. Thanks for calling.'

The idea was to get away from impersonal computer-programmed voices that feature on many automated phone systems and sound about as warm and personal as an I Speak Your Weight machine.

After that Mark went down to the call centre to be given a crash course in using the headset phones. This was to prepare him for an afternoon answering calls from residents and other members of the public. He wanted to see what it was like working at the council coalface, being the public's first point of contact with the council.

According to the staff most of the queries related to uncollected rubbish, stray dogs and cracks in the pavement, but that day the centre was bombarded with calls reporting minor flooding around the city caused by unexpectedly heavy rain. Although the council didn't have unlimited resources and responses had to be prioritised, it was important that callers didn't feel they'd been given the brush-off. There was a real skill in being empathetic and assuring people that their call would be taken seriously, even if the incident they were reporting seemed minor.

What the plumber taught the mayor about business

Towards the end of the shift Mark took a call reporting problems with a water main: there was, apparently, far too much water on the street for it to be solely due to the rain. He recognised the voice on the other end of the line: the caller was a prominent citizen from the northern suburbs who regularly contributed to council business.

Mark noted down the details, sent through an urgent work team request and assured the caller that council staff would be there shortly to address the problem. Without even thinking about it, he added, 'Thanks for your call, Mr Stevens.'

'What?' barked Mr Stevens. 'How did you know my name? Are you tracking this call?'

'I'm sorry, Mr Stevens,' said Mark. 'I just recognised your voice. You were at that public meeting last week about the new park in your suburb.'

'Oh?' said Mr Stevens. 'Have we met?'

'Well, I chaired the meeting. Mark Blumsky's my name; I'm the mayor.'

There was a long pause. 'So why on earth are you answering the phone?'

It was a fair question. Why would the mayor of a capital city spend an afternoon answering the phone? To Mark, it was just a way of doing things, a style of management he'd developed over many years in the retail sector. It had worked for him there and seemed to be serving him well in local government too. He believed people learnt by doing, by getting out in the field and making an effort to understand every aspect of the organisation's operation.

He liked getting out and about, talking to people, watching people. It was the best way to figure out what they were thinking and what they wanted. Talking to customers was the best way of finding out if your advertising was working. Wearing the shoes was the best way of establishing whether they were any good. Working on the shop floor was the most effective way of getting a feel for how the entire operation was running. The best way to learn is to just do it.

Most of his competitors didn't share this hands-on approach. As far as they were concerned, they'd served their apprenticeship and done the hard yards and had no desire to return to the coalface.

In their scheme of things, getting ahead meant getting out of the shop and away from the public and into a wood-panelled office with a comfortable chair and a big desk with a state-of-the-art phone — all the better to harass their underlings. The shop floor was beneath them, literally and metaphorically. Having escaped it, why on earth would they want to go back?

In contrast Mark's philosophy was based on regular

customer contact. It enabled him to keep abreast of their needs and circumstances and, if necessary, adjust the Mischief approach to ensure it fitted with customer expectations.

Trying to do it the other way around — getting customers to adjust their expectations to fit the business's preferred approach — is unsustainable. Sooner rather than later a business will have to fit in with the customers' preferences so it's useful to know what they are.

Shoes to dye for

Mark learned this lesson when he accompanied one of Hannahs' footwear buyers on a series of road shows. Every season the buyers travelled the world evaluating the latest fashion trends and searching out the best products for the chain. They were paid to have their fingers firmly on the fashion pulse and spot the next big thing before everybody else did.

The buyers would purchase the new season's ranges and bring them back to New Zealand to present them to the shop managers and staff. The purpose of the exercise was to give the staff an advance look and feel for the products they'd be selling a few months down the track.

This buyer was an old hand. He'd travelled widely and seen it all. He was convinced that orange and yellow shoes were the next big thing. (This was the early 1990s.) They were huge in Italy and in all the trendy magazines.

At a road show in a small town, the buyer asked the store manager what he thought of this new range. The manager said he liked the shoes but not the colours: his feedback was that the customers still wanted black shoes. They might think the orange and yellow shoes looked cool when they saw them in a magazine, but the bottom line was that black went with everything.

The buyer chuckled at this. The orange and yellow shoes had already been ordered and he was absolutely confident that they'd fly out of this store, just as they'd flown out of stores all over Italy. The manager was unconvinced: just because a product went like a bomb in Italy, that didn't mean it would sell here.

The orange and yellow shoes duly arrived and went on display in the shop window with dramatic effect. Window shoppers would do a double take and come running into the shop.

'Wow, those shoes in the window are amazing. I've seen them in magazines!'

They'd try them on and strut around.

'Awesome! Have you got them in black?'

The manager was right: no matter how entranced they were, people simply wouldn't buy them in orange or yellow.

(Rachel had to confess that she would've been one of those customers who couldn't wait to try on the yellow shoes to see what they looked like on, but wouldn't have bought them in a month of Sundays. Ninety per cent of her shoes were black. It was the safe option.)

There was a postscript to the story. Three months later, Mark was back in that shoe shop helping staff dye the orange and yellow shoes black. It was a long, boring, painstaking process which he wouldn't have had to go through if the buyer had paid attention to the market intelligence provided by a store manager who talked to — and, critically, listened to — his customers every day. The buyer, on the other hand, had been talking to international shoe gurus and reading glossy magazines.

The lesson remained with Mark long after he'd finally removed the last traces of black dye from his hands: stay close to the action. A buyer had to understand the local market as well as keeping his finger on the global pulse. Managers should spend regular time at the coalface to gain a better appreciation of what's really happening.

Shiny happy people

At Mischief there was a constant drive to develop new points of difference. This was a lesson Mark had learned from the plumber.

Mark developed many different initiatives. One successful innovation was the free shoe shine. He hired a couple of students to run a part-time shoe shine stall outside Mischief offering free shoe shines to passers-by. His competitors thought it was crazy; they just couldn't see the point. It was a real hit with the public, though, and the benefit of the feel-good factor created flowed on to Mischief.

There was even a lesson to be learned from the students: they cleaned a lot of shoes and made a bit of money but, importantly, they made their jobs fun. Unprompted, they lived the Mischief philosophy. There was always laughter drifting in from the footpath when they were in action.

The students were crafty too. They'd invite people whose shoes they were shining to take a free lollipop from a big bowl they kept beside their work station. They'd scattered coins around the bowl so when people went to take a lollipop, they'd see the coins, assume they were tips left by previous clients, and feel obliged to match them, even though there wasn't a culture of tipping outside the restaurant industry.

The students were young, smart and had spotted an opportunity that hadn't occurred to Mark. To rub salt into the wound, he was supplying them with the shoe polish and lollipops. Good for them: just quietly, he was actually pleased the students had outsmarted him. They'd displayed exactly the sort of creativity and drive he was looking for in employees.

And they'd given Mark a wake-up call. They'd got away with the little earner on the side because he hadn't followed his own rule, the one about getting to know every aspect of the business by doing it. If he'd spent some time with the students out on the footpath shining shoes, he would've realised what they were up to a lot earlier.

Hidden dangers

While Mark had been painting a very rosy picture of Mischief, he had a warning for Rachel.

While many of Mark's ideas might seem like simple common sense today, that's because our society and culture and way of doing business have moved with the times. Back in the early 1990s, though, these ideas were ahead of their time and amounted to a very novel approach to business.

Mischief had been going brilliantly, selling lots of shoes and retaining staff. The Mischief chain had expanded and there was a real buzz around the stores. People were actually having fun buying shoes and the staff were having fun selling them. It was a magic combination.

Just when things were humming along, just when it seemed that Mischief had found its slippers and the formula was working beautifully, a very real threat emerged. It came out of the blue: in the space of ten minutes dear old Mrs Cummings turned everything upside down.

A kick in the guts

No question about it, Mrs Cummings was Mark's favourite customer and the staff adored her just as much: she was warm and genuine and just a delight to deal with. Mark often used to say that if he had to design the perfect grandmother, he'd just copy Mrs Cummings. She was certainly the honorary granny of the Mischief family.

Despite falling outside Mischief's eighteen to forty-five target demographic, she was the epitome of the loyal customer, buying a pair of shoes a month, regular as clockwork.

She sometimes came in with her daughter. Once, while the staff doted on Mrs Cummings, her daughter told Mark how much the old lady loved her visits to Mischief. Mark was gratified to hear that, but he expressed concern that buying a new pair of shoes every month was an expensive habit for a retiree. Her daughter was quick to assure him that Mrs Cummings could easily afford it. That was good to hear, but he meant what he said when he assured her that Mrs Cummings would always be welcome at Mischief, even if she never spent a cent.

On the fateful day, Mark was watching the world go by through the shop window and reflecting on another good day. He was pleased with how the staff had handled the lunch-hour rush, given that two employees were on leave. As a rule he was reluctant to let two staff take leave at the same time but seeing one was a bride and the other the bridesmaid, he was happy to make an exception.

Half lost in thought, it took him a couple of seconds to register that Mrs Cummings was walking past the window. He waved; she waved back — just as they'd done countless times before. Except it wasn't quite like all those other times:

Slippers: Service and Selling

this time, before she waved back, Mrs Cummings quickly swapped a shopping bag from one hand to the other, as if she didn't want Mark to see it.

But, as if often the case, the furtive movement only drew attention to what it was intended to conceal. Mark had spotted the bag and recognised it instantly: it was from the rival shoe store down the street. His stomach flipped. It really felt like a kick in the guts. As the nausea washed over him, a voice inside his head screamed: *'How could she do that to me?'*

'You saw the bag, didn't you?'

His favourite customer, his best customer, his most loyal customer had bought a pair of shoes from his fiercest rival. He had to know why. Without a word to his staff, he dashed out of the store and, moving in that jerky half-walk, half-run we associate with someone who desperately needs to find a toilet, set off after Mrs Cummings.

Catching up with her was the easy part. Not wanting to come straight out and ask her about the bag and aware that her daughter hadn't been too well, he enquired after the daughter's health. Mrs Cummings assured Mark that her daughter was now fine.

He felt like yelling, 'Well, I'm bloody glad someone is.' He couldn't take his eyes off the rival store's plastic bag. He felt angry and betrayed and, with each passing moment, more of a mind to let Mrs Cummings know that.

There was an uncomfortable silence. Then:

Mrs Cummings:
    I see you've noticed the bag.

Mark: Yes. I'd really like to know — why?

Mrs Cummings:
    I didn't mean to, honestly. I was just walking along the street when this very friendly young woman asked me if I wanted a free shoe shine — she must have noticed my shoes were a bit grubby. So I said yes and followed her into her store. She sat me down and took my shoes off, then a nice young man offered to get me a glass of water.

Mark: Well, it's a warm day so I guess you said yes to that too?

Mrs Cummings:
    Uh-huh. When he brought me the water, he

showed me some shoes that had just come in. Literally — they aren't even on the shelves yet. He asked if I wanted to try them on while my shoes were being cleaned. Well, I wasn't in any great hurry so I did. I must admit I felt a bit special being the first person to try on these shoes. They fitted so well and looked so good and the staff had been so nice to me that, well, I just went ahead and bought them.

Mark: As you do.

Mrs Cummings:

It was only when I saw you waving that it really dawned on me that I hadn't bought them from you. The thing is, it really felt like I was in Mischief. Now I feel terrible. I'm so sorry; I feel like I've let you down.

Mark: You haven't let me down at all. It's not a problem — you're absolutely entitled to buy shoes from wherever you like. To be honest, we've done very well out of you for quite a while now. I bet most of your shoes came from Mischief. So don't you worry about it: enjoy your new shoes and have a lovely afternoon. And thank you — and I mean that sincerely.

Mrs Cummings was a bit taken aback but Mark meant exactly what he'd said. While he was mortified at the turn of events, now that he'd calmed down and was thinking more clearly, he was grateful to her for teaching him a valuable lesson and annoyed with himself for having had to learn it the hard way.

The cold, hard fact of the matter was that Mischief Shoes was no longer different. His competitors had seen how well Mischief's innovative approach was working and had unashamedly copied it. Mark's shops were now just like all the others. It had taken Mrs Cummings and her plastic bag to show him that he'd lost his slippers.

Don't believe your own hype

Mischief had become a victim of its own success. Success had bred complacency, even arrogance. They were so wrapped up in being named Retailer of the Year and being interviewed by the media and patting themselves on the back that they'd stopped taking notice of what was happening around them and particularly what the competition was up to. Their rivals hadn't made that mistake. They'd studied his operation in detail, copied the things that had made Mischief successful, and now they were stealing his business. That's how business works.

When someone comes up with a good idea, they have only a limited window of opportunity in which to exploit that edge because it's only a matter of time before his competitors replicate it. Imitation might be the sincerest form of flattery, but in business it hits you where it hurts — smack in the bottom line.

Mischief had revolutionised shoe retailing, but Mark should have realised that his lead over the chasing pack wouldn't last forever. Mischief had found its slippers and then stood still. And guess what? The market had caught up. That's what happens in a competitive system. Now every shop was doing the lollipops, the funky music and the free shoe shines.

What had once been new was now old. What had been points of difference were now standard industry practice. Mark had made the fundamental mistake of underestimating his competition and assuming that they wouldn't change and adapt to meet the challenge he'd set.

Now habit was the only reason for Mrs Cummings to patronise Mischief rather than a number of other shoe stores. What really worried Mark was that if his number one customer could be lured away, how many others had been lost? Could Mischief no longer count on customer loyalty and the repeat business it generated?

This state of affairs wasn't going to go away or fix itself. Something had to be done and quickly. The first step was to sit down with his staff and talk about what they could do to win back people like Mrs Cummings.

The question was how and when could he get everyone together? People had commitments after work — study, family, boyfriends and girlfriends, sport, to name but a few. The solution was to take all the staff away on a weekend retreat: it would double as a team-building exercise, and there'd be nothing to distract them from the quest to rediscover Mischief's slippers.

The retreat — Day One

One Saturday a few weeks later, Mark closed the stores early. All the staff met at the main store and got on a bus. When he devised the format for the retreat, Mark settled on three rules which he believed would be critical to the weekend's success. The first rule of the retreat was that everyone attended, right down to the part-timers who worked after school and the students who operated the shoe shine. Mark rang the parents of the younger staff to brief them about the retreat and assure them their children would be well looked after and would benefit from the experience.

The venue for the retreat was a seaside resort. To put it another way, it was a pretty basic motor camp not far from the sea. More to the point, it was easily the cheapest place to put up twenty people for a weekend within two hours of the capital. The rooms were functional but clean and there was a conference room that was just big enough for the group. The decor was seventies take-us-as-you-find-us with mismatched tables and chairs and plastic orange light shades. But there was a whiteboard and a pool so all in all it was ideal for a company that couldn't afford to splash money around.

After unpacking, they got straight down to business, assembling in the conference room where Mark set the scene.

Most of the staff had heard the story about Peter the Plumber when they started with Mischief, but Mark took them through it again to remind them of the slippers message and how integral it was to the Mischief concept. He stressed the importance of the vision and points of difference Mischief had developed by following the plumber's lead. Judging by their reaction, most of the staff were aware of the part slippers had played in their success.

He then told them why Mrs Cummings had bought shoes from the competitor down the road. The smiles faded. By the time Mark finished his opening remarks, no one in the room was under any illusions: the company was at the crossroads; if changes weren't made, its future was uncertain.

The plan was to start with a no-holds-barred session in which ideas for change would be written up on the whiteboard and discussed. This was where the second rule came into effect: every single idea went up on the board, no matter who it came from or how outrageous or idiotic it seemed at first sight.

The session took a while to get going, but eventually ideas started to flow:

Senior salesman:
>Why don't we give people orange juice instead of water?

Mark: I like it. It would certainly be more colourful. Pure fruit juice is expensive, though. It might have to be those mixes you add water to.

Shoe shiner:
>We should give them something healthier than lollipops — grapes, for instance.

Mark: Well, people are getting more health conscious. The pips would be a pain, as would sourcing them fresh every day. But I'm sure we can find a way.

Junior saleswoman: When someone buys a pair of men's business shoes, we could give them a back-up set of laces in case the originals break.

Mark: Nice one. Half the blokes who come in have got broken laces.

After-school part-timer: Why don't we try never to make mistakes? And if we do stuff up, we give the customer money.

Mark: You're joking, right? That's insane. We can't start giving customers money every time something goes wrong.

ASPT: Why not?

Mark: Because the accountant would have a heart attack.

ASPT: Mark, that's not fair. You said all ideas, no matter how off-the-wall, would go on the whiteboard. Now you're changing your tune.

Mark: Fair call. Up it goes. Okay, what's next?

Senior saleswoman:
>Stiletto heels: the tips on the heels are always wearing out or breaking. We could fix them for nothing, at least the first time. It doesn't take long and wouldn't cost that much.

Mark: Yeah, that'd be popular.

Trainee salesman:
>What about free mints?

Senior salesman:
>That's worse than lollipops. Besides, mints have already been used.

Mark: Everything goes on the board — that's the rule.

Junior salesman:
>How about a free pair of sports socks with every pair of sports shoes?

Mark: Makes sense. It would certainly go down well.

Top salesman:
>Here's an idea: if a couple comes in and they both buy shoes, they get a double pass to a movie.

Mark: Nice idea; very romantic. We could make it a condition that they have to wear their new shoes to the movie.

Slippers: Service and Selling

ASPT: What if it's a parent and child? Could the parent give their pass to someone else?
Mark: How would we stop them?

As the session continued, everyone entered into the spirit of things. People were trying to outdo each other in creative thinking and come up with the knockout idea. It didn't take long for the whiteboard to fill up so another one had to be brought in. By the end of the session that was full of ideas too. Some ideas were great, some were okay and a few were just plain ridiculous, but the rule stipulated that they all went up on the whiteboard.

What the plumber taught the mayor about business

It had been a long day of work, travel and brainstorming, but the Mischief team was still fizzing. They were sure that somewhere hidden in among the scrawl on the two whiteboards recording their outpouring of ideas and innovation was the new slippers. The action switched to the pool, which provided a useful outlet for the surplus energy and pent-up excitement. Everyone ended up getting wet, whether they wanted to or not and whether they'd taken the precaution of getting into their swimming gear or not.

The retreat — Day Two

The next day's session started a bit later than planned. Looking around the room, Mark could see that some of the staff were a little the worse for wear. He consoled himself with the thought that hangovers were part and parcel of team building.

The object of the second session was to whittle down the ideas on the whiteboards. With the best will in the world, there was no way Mischief could implement all of them. The aim was to find the new slippers — a slippers that would withstand the test of time and, more importantly, the competitors' response.

This was where the third and final rule came in: if the shop down the road, especially the one that enticed dear old Mrs Cummings, could easily copy the idea, it would be wiped off the board and forgotten about. This whole exercise had come about because rival shoe stores had shown they were ready, willing and able to steal good ideas, so the bar had to be set high. The search was on for ideas that no one else would or could mimic.

The orange juice was wiped — anyone could do that.

The grapes were wiped — if Mischief could overcome the difficulties of getting them in fresh every day, so could the opposition.

Mints were wiped — restaurants were doing them.

Laces were wiped — shoe shops generally had a pretty good supply of laces on hand, so it would be a piece of cake to replicate.

Free re-heeling was wiped — most shoe shops did that already, especially if the shoes were quite new.

Sports socks were wiped — there was already a glut of promotional socks in the market.

Even the movie passes got wiped — it didn't take much discussion to establish that the hassles would outweigh the gains.

After two hours of animated debate and ruthless

weeding-out, there was only one idea left. It was the craziest one of all, the one that was going to cause the accountant to have a seizure:

'If we stuff up, we give the customer money.'
'If we stuff up, we give the customer money.'
'If we stuff up, we give the customer money.'

The reason it was the only idea to survive the cull was simple: there was unanimous agreement that Mischief's competitors would have to be nuts to copy it. Of course, you didn't have to be a professor of logic to figure out that if they'd have to be nuts to copy it, Mischief would have to be nuts to do it in the first place.

Nevertheless, it was the only idea left on the board, the only one that met the strict qualification. Could it be done? How would it work? Was it financially feasible? Who was going to break the news to the accountant?

Mark challenged the staff to find a way to make it work. They'd put so much time and effort and energy into generating ideas, it would be a real anticlimax if the idea that emerged from their brainstorming ended up in the too-hard basket. His warning that giving away money would be a very hard sell to the accountant made them realise that the challenge was largely one of packaging: they needed to translate the idea into a practical, workable, interesting format while preserving its essential audacity or insanity, depending on your point of view.

Someone suggested that rather than dishing out money in the event of a stuff-up, the customer could receive a gift voucher. That immediately put the idea on a more practical footing. A voucher that was redeemable only in a Mischief store kept the business within the chain and reduced the real cost to about half the face value of the voucher.

More problematical was defining what counted as a stuff-up. What if there was a power cut so customers couldn't actually see the shoes on their feet? Did that count? What if the courier bringing the shoes from another store delivered a day late? Whose fault was it if the customer insisted that the shoes were a perfect fit but discovered when wearing them the next day that they were too big or too small?

What 'stuffing up' really means

Mark agreed that defining what was and wasn't a stuff-up was a tricky matter, but it was critical to the whole exercise and, what's more, it had to be done there and then. They weren't leaving the motor camp until it was resolved: in fact, if it came to that, he'd lock them in the conference room until they came up with a solution.

For their part the staff were keen to come up with a definition that was strict and narrow, and which limited liability to situations over which they had some control. They didn't want to be penalised for other people's mistakes, such as having to hand out vouchers because a construction contractor working two blocks away sliced through a cable. The scene was set for a long, intense debate over exactly what constituted a stuff-up.

The after-school part-timer who'd come up with the original idea also hit upon the idea of using the Ten out of Ten model as the basis for the debate. Everyone was familiar with it and used to putting it into practice. It was built into their training and a source of pride and satisfaction in the shop. Once they'd settled on that, it was a matter of determining whether all ten principles would apply or whether the list should be pared back to the most relevant and practical.

Mark sat back and let them fight it out. They went through them one at a time. After an exhaustive review, only five were deemed applicable. If any of these five undertakings were not delivered, it would constitute a stuff-up and the customer would receive a gift voucher.

The final rules around vouchers for stuff-ups were:

1. Mischief staff didn't ask customers, 'Can I help you?' If they did, the customer would get a $100 gift voucher.
2. The Mischief experience entailed staff helping — or at least offering to help — every customer to put their shoes on. Not doing so would mean a $100 gift voucher.
3. Mischief believed it was important that customers were advised how to keep their new shoes cleaned and maintained because it showed the shop wanted them to get maximum value out of their purchase. If this wasn't done, the customer would receive a $100 gift voucher.
4. Mischief staff were trained to tell customers what materials their new shoes were made of. If this didn't happen at the point of sale, the customer would get a $100 gift voucher.
5. People liked to know which country their shoes came from. If this information wasn't provided, they would now receive a $100 gift voucher.

The five stuff-up rules, which essentially reflected staff

training and were part of the Mischief experience, became the Mischief Guarantee.

 A new beginning

It was a weary Mischief team who travelled back to Wellington late on the Sunday afternoon. Even so, Mark sensed they were looking forward to the challenges ahead. The new slippers wouldn't be phased in over weeks or months; Mischief really did change overnight because the decisions made at the retreat were implemented the very next day.

The shoes on display in the shop window were removed and replaced with a large notice announcing the new guarantee and listing each of the five stuff-ups. The information was also displayed on smaller signs placed around the store.

The guarantee was brought to the public's attention through a comprehensive — and humorous — newspaper and radio advertising campaign. Straight away people began popping into the store in the hope that one of the staff would ask, 'Can I help you?'

The Mischief buzz was back.
The point of difference was back.
Slippers were back.

Why it worked

Six months later, one of Mark's regular customers asked him how much the guarantee had cost. Seeing he prefaced the question by observing that the Mischief stores always seemed busy, he was obviously expecting a hair-raising figure. Needless to say, he was stunned when Mark informed him that despite the thousands of customers who'd been through the Mischief stores since the guarantee was introduced, they'd given away a grand total of five vouchers. When the customer expressed amazement, Mark explained how they'd come up with the initiative and pointed out that it was essentially an extension of the Mischief shopping experience concept which formed the core of his staff training.

The customer's wife, who'd overheard the discussion, reckoned the initiative's success owed far more to the fact that the staff owned the idea than to their training. She argued that the staff's enthusiasm and commitment was a direct result of the process: because they'd driven it, they felt a sense of ownership, rather than seeing it as being imposed from above, without consultation.

Looking back on it, Mark agrees. It was the staff's idea from start to finish. Both the concept of the guarantee and the five stuff-ups were created and developed by the staff. They were proud of it and, more importantly, proud of the positive impact it was having on the business.

New staff members picked up the concept quickly and became quite protective of it. No one wanted to compromise Mischief's reputation for delivering on its guarantee. As a result, Ten out of Ten became even more ingrained in the Mischief culture. The staff weren't content just to deliver on the five points that ensured there was no need to hand out a voucher; they worked just as hard on the other five.

Capturing all the ideas

Mischief experienced spectacular growth over the next two years, essentially because Mark had — after some prompting — agreed to consider an idea from a schoolgirl who worked part time. This proved to him that excellent ideas can come from anywhere in the organisation. The corollary is that management doesn't have a monopoly on good ideas.

Mark's first instinct had been to dismiss the idea out of hand because, at first blush, it seemed so completely off the wall. Luckily for him, the part-timer had stuck to her guns and reminded him why he'd come up with Rule Two — that every idea, no matter how outrageous, goes up on the whiteboard — in the first place. If he hadn't backed down, he would've missed out on the concept which revitalised his business.

The lesson Mark learned from this was that a truly innovative organisation uses all the talents of all its staff. Creativity doesn't follow an organisational chart. A good idea is a good idea regardless of what level the person who came up with it is on or what their title is.

Bottling the lightning

Sadly that epic whiteboard session can't be replicated because the motor camp no longer does corporate retreats.

Maybe some of the furniture that ended up in the pool had sentimental value for the camp's owner.

However, the key to the weekend's success — and Mischief's subsequent growth — wasn't the location but the three rules adopted at the outset. These rules have universal application so they could be used by any organisation or business in any field of activity:

Rule 1: Everyone in the organisation or company attends. All staff members, regardless of status or experience, must be made to feel that their contribution is as valued as the next person's and encouraged to contribute freely, as equals.

Rule 2: In the first session, all ideas from all sources are written up on the whiteboard. Nothing is ruled out as too impractical, expensive or outrageous because ideas which at first sight seem absurd can sometimes be refined into something workable and powerful.

Rule 3: In the second session, any idea which can be copied by competitors is ruthlessly discarded. If not, you'll be back at the camp repeating the process sooner rather than later.

'Thanks for buying a $400,000 house — have a $4 box of chocolates'

Another regular customer was a real estate agent whose son had worked part time at Mischief while at university. In fact the son had attended the weekend retreat and later told his father about the whiteboard sessions and how they'd generated the idea that had revitalised Mischief.

Intrigued, the agent asked Mark for more information. Rather than talk him through it, Mark offered to show him by running a similar session for the real estate company. Yes, footwear and real estate seemed poles apart but Mark was confident the methodology could work whatever the product or service.

Not long afterwards, the staff of the real estate firm assembled in a conference room at a local hotel on a midweek night. Mark told them of his encounter with Peter the Plumber and explained how the Mischief guarantee had been created. He spelt out the three rules and outlined how he hoped the session would unfold.

He shared a personal experience of the real estate industry. He'd been house-hunting and was particularly taken by one property because it was so beautifully furnished. When he told the agent he was under the impression that the occupants had already moved out, the agent admitted they were long gone: all the nice touches — the art on the walls, the lovely furniture and the fresh flowers — would come out of his commission. He'd hired them because an empty, unfurnished house was a much harder sell. It was, he confided, an old trick but everyone did it — because it worked.

This was demonstrated yet again a few days later when Mark bought the house. Even though he knew what the agent was up to, it didn't deter Mark. What he'd seen on that first visit had left an indelible favourable impression: he'd been able to see the house's potential. If the house had been empty, it would have seemed cold and unwelcoming and almost certainly left him unimpressed.

Before he called for their ideas for the whiteboard, Mark challenged the agents to think creatively and come up with a similarly effective idea, but one that couldn't be copied by everybody in the industry.

There was no shortage of ideas. The whiteboard filled up rapidly, mostly with variations on the giveaway: bottles of wine, cleaning vouchers, food hampers, pot plants, chocolates.

When the whiteboard was full, Mark made them review their suggestions. When subjected to scrutiny, it quickly became apparent that most of the ideas were either easily copied or in fact already being used by some of their competitors. Adopting them wouldn't establish a genuine point of difference; it would only make them even less distinguishable from the competition. One by one they were erased until the whiteboard was white again.

Back to the whiteboard

The real estate agents started again. There was no shortage of determination to find a point of difference from every other real estate company in town. After all, wanting to be different was the reason they'd left other companies and joined together to create their own. When an office junior reminded the group that their task was to 'Find their slippers', Mark knew they'd got the concept and it was only a matter of time before they found what they were looking for.

Things took a promising turn when one of the newer agents mentioned what a difference gardens can make. She'd missed out on a sale that afternoon because the potential buyer, who'd seemed very keen, got hung up on the fact that the garden needed weeding and lawn was overdue a mow. Even though these were superficial things that could be easily remedied, she had to admit they made the property look rundown and she could see why the potential buyer had been turned off.

The others agreed — an attractive garden can create a good first impression. Just as we're quick to form impressions of other people when meeting them for the first time, so too with houses, and a nice garden was a key part of that 'moment of truth'. It made a house easier to sell and often pushed up the price. There was such a strong consensus on the value of a garden that it begged the question: could they somehow develop the garden theme into their point of difference?

It was the quietest agent, the sort who sits in a corner listening intently but seldom volunteering an opinion, who suggested they should do the gardening themselves. That met with swift and vehement opposition from the older agents who made it crystal clear that yanking weeds out of someone else's garden wasn't their idea of a fun weekend. The quiet bloke said that wasn't what he meant: he reckoned the company should buy a truck and employ gardeners to look after all the properties on their books.

It was the Eureka! moment.

They'd get a gardening truck and proudly but tastefully brand it as their very own new and exclusive gardening service.

The gardeners would do the rounds of the houses on their books, ensuring that the lawns and gardens were a picture. When not in use, the truck would function as a mobile billboard, to be parked outside one of their immaculate properties. It would send a clear message to potential sellers that this real estate company was prepared to go the extra mile to sell houses for the best price, thereby helping to attract exclusive listings.

It wasn't all talk. The company ran with the idea and had their best year ever. There was no doubt that that gardening service was a huge success and a decisive factor in the company's surge to becoming the market leader.

Ultimately, any point of difference can be copied if the competitor has the resources and the determination not to be left behind. Mark warned the agents that their edge was unlikely to last indefinitely. The more success they had with it, the nearer they'd be to the day when a competitor introduced its own version of the gardening service. That was simply the way business worked. If they wanted to remain number one, they would have to continue to innovate.

Rachel's feedback

A couple of weeks after the second extended conversation, Rachel buttonholed Mark as he was cooling down from his workout. Ever since he'd told her about the plumber's slippers, she said, she'd been evaluating her shopping experiences and assessing the various retail outlets she patronised with a fresh perspective. There were times when she almost wished she'd never heard of Peter the Plumber and Mischief because she now zeroed in on things she'd previously barely noticed or shrugged off. To cut a long story short, so many of the shops she went into were in dire need of one of Mark's makeovers.

Some of the service she'd encountered was beyond bad; it was shocking. How did they expect to make money? Furthermore, no one seemed to be having fun. It was nothing like the Mischief experience that Mark had described.

Mark had to agree. He saw a lot of businesses, not all of them retailers, which were barely at first base in terms of providing proper customer service. The good news was that it wasn't a hard thing to fix. One of the most effective and easiest ways for businesses to run a reality check on where their company is at is to visit other businesses to see how they operate and experience their service at first hand. You very quickly get a sense of what they're doing differently and whether or not it's working.

Mark believed so strongly in the value of this sort of reconnaissance that it had become a feature of Mischief's induction programme.

Sleeping with one eye open

Mischief shoes had regained its slippers. People loved the guarantee and were always keen to put the staff to the test, even though they never seemed to score a voucher. And in turn the staff took a lot of pride in protecting 'their' record and 'their' idea.

It always made Mark smile to see yet another customer trying to trick the staff — they usually went for the younger ones — into saying, 'Can I help you?' The staff developed an acute sense of when a customer was angling for a voucher — they tended to prowl the store as if searching for an opening.

In fact sometimes the staff would just walk right up to them and cheerfully announce, 'I'm not going to say it, you

What the plumber taught the mayor about business

know.' This usually met with feigned ignorance: 'Say what?' 'The hundred-dollar words.' The customer would continue to pretend they were blissfully ignorant of the guarantee or how you qualified for it right up until they walked out of the store with a new pair of shoes.

Mark was delighted with how things had turned out: he'd recognised that he had a problem, he'd come up with a plan to address it and the plan had worked. Thanks to the new point of difference, Mischief was going great guns.

But business being business, he still fretted about his

competitors. He knew they were watching his stores — the Mrs Cummings incident had proved that. Maybe it was time to turn the tables and start watching them.

Every new Mischief staff member was given a buddy on day one, an experienced staff member to teach them the Mischief Way — and a few tricks of the trade. During the first seven days of training the buddy stuck to the newbie like glue. Checking out the competition was part of that training: the newbies went around town peering into shoe store windows, ostensibly window-shopping but in reality getting a feel for who the opposition was and how they operated.

Mark decided to take it a step further. He decided that rather than window-shop, newbies would spend their first day on the Mischief payroll in — as opposed to outside — rival shoe stores. They would be paid to go shoe shopping.

Of course, they weren't encouraged to actually buy anything. The idea was that they'd go into the other shoe shops, have a good browse and try on a few pairs of shoes, all the while keeping a sharp eye on the product range and the service. And if they timed their visits for the busiest times of the day, particularly lunch hour, they could observe how their counterparts dealt with pressure.

The next day the newbies would give a short presentation to their colleagues outlining what they'd learned and submit a written report, which Mark kept for future reference.

Although a tad sneaky, this scheme had a number of advantages:

- Because the 'spy' had never actually worked in a Mischief store, the other shops had no way of knowing they were being 'spied' on.
- Because the newbies hadn't had any sales training, they had no preconceived ideas or expectations about how staff in shoe stores should operate.
- Their reports provided a steady flow of unfiltered and honest market intelligence from a customer's perspective.

It meant that Mischief was never taking its eyes off the opposition. The company knew what each of its rivals was doing well, what it wasn't doing so well and what it was doing badly. Mark could keep track of any changes and innovations his rivals introduced and would get to know pretty quickly if Mischief initiatives were being copied. (Along the way he picked up on one or two things worth copying.) Finally, the newbies got something of a crash course in the industry by putting themselves in the customer's shoes for a day.

Are you being served?

Sometimes the 'spies' returned to base bewildered or even angry at the treatment they'd received. Over time Mark assembled a bulging file of horror stories about what passed for customer service in some shoe outlets:

- 'I haven't got a clue what their service is like because the staff completely ignored me. I guess I looked like I couldn't afford the shoes.'
- 'Everything was difficult for this guy. He acted like wanting to try on a pair of shoes before buying them was completely unreasonable. Doesn't everyone do that?'
- 'The salesperson said all the right things but the body language — sighing and shrugging his shoulders — whenever I asked a question put me off.'
- 'When I asked about a pair of shoes, they seemed relieved that they didn't have them. They just turned and walked off. It was like "Thank God for that." Obviously, they were far more focused on their lunch break and I was only going to hold them up.'
- 'I got asked "Can I help you?" This salesperson then went around the store asking everyone else the same

question. It was liked being served by a robot.'
- 'Four different staff members asked me "Are you okay there?" I was beginning to get a complex. I wanted to rush to a mirror to see if I looked ill. It seemed a strange way to try to start a conversation.'
- 'I never realised what a barrier the counter is. The staff wouldn't come out from behind it. I felt like I was the enemy.'
- 'The guy seemed nice. He asked me how my day was going, showed me some shoes, then asked me again how my day was going. He was obviously on auto-pilot, asking every customer the same question but having absolutely zero interest in their answers.'
- 'There was plenty of staff there, but they were all too busy doing something on the computer to actually help anyone.'
- 'The guy behind the counter didn't know if the shoes I wanted were in stock, so he just yelled to someone out the back. It was like he was chained to his desk. He's probably still there.'
- 'I actually got told off for picking up a shoe. Apparently you can only touch a shoe once you've decided you're definitely going to buy it.'
- 'The staff member assigned to my part of the store wouldn't get off the phone even though there were people waiting. Her mum's obviously their best customer.'

- 'The two staff in the shop were too busy discussing their weekend. Admittedly, there was a hell of a lot to discuss, most of it X-rated. I started to feel nauseous as well as ignored so I left.'

Many of the new staff vowed not to make the same mistakes. They'd been on the receiving end and didn't like it. There was no better way for them to learn about service than by spending some time in the customer's shoes.

Rachel's inevitable question

By this stage Mark and Rachel had had several long conversations on the broad subject of the Mark Blumsky Business Philosophy of Doing Business so what came next was inevitable. She prefaced it by saying she was going to ask an impertinent question so she'd understand if he didn't want to answer it, but it was something which had been on her mind since Mark first told her about Mischief.

'Given that you'd built Mischief into a busy little footwear empire, why didn't you just carry on, make your millions and retire at forty? Why on earth would you decide to run for the mayoralty and expose yourself to all the hassles and stress of local politics?'

It was a good question. The answer was that Mark hadn't gone out on his own in order to get rich quick. He wanted to create a different sort of shoe store and a new style of doing business, incorporating the lessons he'd learned from Peter the Plumber. Above all, he'd wanted to use the slippers concept to create a retail leader.

He'd achieved those goals; the plumber's model had worked. By giving Mischief its slippers, Mark had managed to create a very successful footwear operation.

But despite, or perhaps because of, Mischief's success, Mark reached a stage where he needed a new challenge. He began to think about the bigger picture.

Looking towards the bigger picture

Mischief's growth and expansion meant that Mark wasn't nearly as involved in day-to-day work and fire-fighting — in short, not as hands-on — as he'd been previously. There was no need: sales were up, the staff were operating as a team and achieving consistent Ten out of Tens, and everyone seemed to be having fun. The formula was working.

While he missed the engagement and personal contact, his changed circumstances did allow him to address some of the business issues that were impacting on his business and had serious implications for its future.

All the Mischief stores were in the city centre. The problem was that all stores in the city shut quite early on Saturday afternoon and didn't open on Sundays, which was a massive disincentive to go shopping in town at the weekend. Why bother going into town when everything shut down just as the credit card was getting warmed up? To make matters worse, if you drove in, you got hit with very high street parking fees.

By contrast, Mischief's competitors out in the suburban shopping malls were open for most of the weekend within a short walk of acres of free parking. So for half of Saturday and all of Sunday, Mark was paying rent on shops that weren't even open for business while his suburban competitors were flat out. Clearly, if they'd had the choice, some of those weekend shoe buyers would have preferred going to a Mischief store, but that option wasn't available. Mark saw this as a real problem and resolved to do something about it.

He lobbied other central Wellington retailers to extend

Saturday opening hours until four o'clock and floated the idea of opening on Sundays. His argument was that if all shops were open, people would start coming back into town because of the greater choice and convenience. Most of the other retailers thought it sounded like a good idea but were sceptical. Would shoppers actually come back into town? Wouldn't they be put off by the cost of parking?

Their reservations were entirely reasonable. If they opened their stores and no one came, they were going to lose a lot of money.

Breaking the cycle

It was a catch-22: no one came because nothing was open; nothing was open because no one came. The situation needed a circuit breaker to wean the retailers off the habit of basically giving the game away at lunchtime on Saturday.

Mark sat down with the Wellington City Council to find a way to bring shoppers back to the city. They concluded that an orchestrated marketing campaign was probably the best method: the inner city would be marketed as if it was a shopping mall. Discussions were held on reducing or even eliminating the high parking charges which put the centre of town at such a disadvantage relative to the suburbs.

Several months went by: months crammed with meetings, discussions, handshakes and paperwork. But despite all the good intentions and fine words no real progress was made on the substantive issues, nothing concrete had been put in place to resolve the catch-22. Frustrated, Mark fired off a strongly worded letter to the mayor and the city's chief executive asking if the council was really committed to the cause.

The eventual council response was to put the ball firmly back in Mark's court: if he could demonstrate that other city retailers supported the idea, the council might come on board. Mark's first step towards making this happen was to bring together like-minded businesses on a committee which would market and promote the city.

The committee wrote to every retail business in the central city asking them to compete with the suburban shopping centres by opening at the weekend. They were also asked to pay a levy to fund marketing, advertising and on-street activity to support the weekend opening campaign. Quite a few retailers signed up; many chose not to.

Armed with a fighting fund, the committee organised a razzmatazz event backed up by an advertising blitz to launch weekend shopping in the city. The launch was a noisy, busy, buzzing, hugely successful event with a 'fun for all the family' feel to it. Several streets were closed off to create recreational spaces and provide plenty of room for the various activities. There were buskers, bands, food stalls, competitions and other street entertainment. Virtually every retailer opened and shoppers came out in force.

Mark was a bit irked to see that many of the stores which had declined to back the campaign or contribute to the levy were cashing in on the launch. They were more than happy to reap the rewards of the huge interest and high turnout generated by the work and promotional expenditure of the committee and its supporters.

The main thing, though, was that weekend shopping in the inner city was now up and running.

'If you don't like it . . .'

Although delighted with the success of the launch and the campaign, Mark was well aware that a voluntary levy would not sustain the level of promotion that was needed over the long term. He asked the council to consider a compulsory levy or, alternatively, provide a grant to cover future costs.

Neither of those measures aroused much interest or enthusiasm among council staff. In fact, a senior council officer told Mark, partly in jest, that if he didn't like the way the council operated, he should run for the mayoralty. Mark laughed it off. He assumed it was the staff's standard smart-arse response to anyone who complained about the council.

But a seed had been planted. The idea of standing for mayor was now lodged in Mark's head and wouldn't go away. Mischief was going great guns — so great in fact that he was in danger of becoming bored. There wasn't the same challenge any more. He no longer leapt out of bed energised at the prospect of heading off to work; he worried that his declining enthusiasm might prove contagious and drag the rest of his team down. He'd always believed in leading by example and displaying a supercharged attitude that permeated the organisation. If his attitude was no longer super — and he knew it wasn't — perhaps it was time to take on a new challenge.

Aim high

Contesting an election, winning the mayoralty and bringing meaningful change to such a large, entrenched institution was undoubtedly a dauntingly challenging prospect. On the plus side, the retirement of the incumbent created a definite window of opportunity. Mark would be competing on a level playing field, as opposed to taking on a well-known figure who had all the advantages that go with being the sitting mayor. After talking it over with family and friends, he decided to give it a go.

The twist was that he wouldn't be running for the council: it would be the mayoralty or bust. His thinking was that if he was going to take a shot at local politics, he might as well aim high. There was only so much he could do as just another councillor. The aim of the exercise was to be an agent for change, to bring about a genuine cultural shift. To do that, he needed to be the boss.

All told, thirteen runners lined up at the start line and the crowded field included some highly credentialed candidates — well-known figures in the business world, former Members of Parliament, community leaders, sitting councillors and a few hardy perennials.

The media didn't take Mark's candidacy seriously because he'd never run for, let alone held, political office. As far as the self-appointed experts of the fourth estate were concerned, his achievements in business were irrelevant: when all was said and done, he was a shoe salesman and what would a shoe salesman know about running a capital city? Early on when the newspapers bothered to mention him at all, the name of his fictional counterpart Al Bundy usually popped up in the same sentence. It would be safe to say that *Married With Children* is Mark's all-time least favourite TV show.

Being dismissed by the press didn't dent Mark's confidence. He believed that winning an election, like succeeding in business, was all about creating a point of difference. This would be doubly true given the number of candidates. He also hoped to leverage off Mischief by tapping into the goodwill of the thousands of customers he'd dealt with over the years.

Besides, Mark had a secret weapon — slippers. He knew the advantage of having a clear vision; he'd seen how well it had worked for Peter the Plumber and Mischief Shoes. The trick was to do something similar, but in the supposedly very different environment of a political campaign.

His campaign began to develop momentum during the public meetings. All the other candidates looked and sounded the same: serious to a fault. They wanted to talk about the city's finances, yearly plans, rates, footpaths, road works, sewerage . . . While these things are all important in their way and therefore worthy of discussion, there has to be more to a city than a balance sheet, holes in the road and drains. There was no spark and, crucially, no point of difference. None of the other candidates had their slippers. They were all wearing practical but boring grey shoes.

The image problem

Much to the surprise of the Wellington political establishment, the shoe salesman turned out to have a very clear grasp of the main issue confronting the capital city. Wellington had a serious image problem. The rest of the country saw the city as being cold, windy and boring. The celebrated poet James K. Baxter once called it the 'sterile whore of a thousand bureaucrats'.

What made it all the more depressing was that, as many Wellingtonians knew in their heart of hearts, this lousy reputation wasn't entirely unjustified, although the bureaucracy had expanded dramatically since Baxter wrote his poem.

Oh no, not Wellington!

It was the stewardesses who made Mark realise just what a negative impression people had of the capital city. He'd won the account to provide footwear for the staff of a regional airline so there was a steady flow of stewardesses and airline counter staff coming into Mischief. They tended to be bubbly personalities, exactly the sort of customers he wanted to have — and to be seen — in the store. Now and again, though, one of them would show up in a dark mood and it was usually because they had to go to Auckland for the day.

The first few times Mark heard this explanation, he didn't have much of a reaction beyond thinking 'Rather you than me.' He assumed most Wellingtonians shared his view of Auckland as a glorified car park, so why wouldn't they be grumpy? As it turned out, the problem with going to Auckland wasn't actually Auckland.

The problem was Wellington. The stewardesses were going to Auckland to work at the Mystery Weekend counter at the airport. Usually given as gifts, a Mystery Weekend voucher entitled the bearer to a return flight to somewhere on the domestic network. As the name suggests, the destination was selected at random. When the travellers turned up at the airport an hour before departure, they were handed an envelope containing their tickets. Then, and only then, did they find out where they'd be spending the weekend away they were so looking forward to.

The trouble started when the travellers opened their

envelope and found out they were going to Wellington. Hardly anyone wanted to go there. They wanted to go to Rotorua or Christchurch or Napier or Queenstown — anywhere but the capital. Wellington was not considered an attractive or cool destination; indeed as far as the disgruntled travellers were concerned, it was pretty much bereft of redeeming features. However, the tickets were completely non-negotiable and non-transferable — it was Wellington or nowhere. The deflated or irate travellers tended to vent their feelings on the nearest target who, of course, was the poor stewardess who'd handed them the envelope.

Mark decided that his main aim as mayor would be to

make people want to come to Wellington. He wanted them to open the envelope with their fingers crossed that the destination on the ticket would be the capital city.

He came up with the slogan 'Send Yourself to Wellington'. If he could make that slogan resonate around the country, he would've fixed the problem, and working on the Mystery Weekend desk would be a pleasure.

During the campaign, Mark told the stewardess story at every opportunity. It was a simple but very effective way of getting across to the public why he was running for mayor and what he hoped to achieve if he got the job. The voters could relate to it — they all knew people who had a negative view of their city.

That story became a significant point of difference. 'Send Yourself to Wellington' became the basis of Mark's vision for Wellington.

A city is more than a balance sheet

Mark differentiated himself clearly from the other candidates by focusing on quite different issues. He wanted to be identified as the positive candidate, the one with a sense of fun and pride who got people excited about their city and what it could become.

At most of the public meetings, the thirteen candidates had just three minutes to deliver their message. It wasn't a long time to create an impression and secure votes. Once you'd covered rates, dogs, rubbish, footpaths and drains there wasn't much time for anything else or much scope for setting yourself apart from the other candidates.

Mark focused on just four issues, all of which linked in to his vision of 'Send Yourself to Wellington'.

1. City shops to open at the weekend because the city centre needed to be vibrant and busy 24/7.
2. Free parking in the city at weekends to help retailers and the hospitality industry entice shoppers into town.
3. More cultural, social and sporting events in the city to give people even more of a reason to visit the city, especially at weekends.
4. Work to start on creating a world-class stadium to enable the city to host national and international sports and entertainment events which would attract visitors to the city.

The key was to attract locals and visitors into the city at weekends and ensure that they enjoyed themselves when they were there. That meant entertainment and a wide range of retail, dining and hospitality options.

The four policies had the common theme of getting people to want to come to Wellington.

The vision thing

The early opinion polls confirmed that these issues were striking a chord with voters who were looking at someone with a positive — even supercharged — attitude to get the city moving. That gave Mark confidence that voters were responding to his vision and that he'd successfully created the point of difference needed to set him apart from the other candidates.

To the surprise of the pundits and in defiance of conventional political wisdom, Mark Blumsky won the 1995 Wellington mayoral election by a comfortable margin.

Clearly, Mark's vision couldn't be implemented overnight, but he was determined that, as mayor, he'd assess every decision he had to make for its potential impact on his vision. Will doing this make people more willing to come to Wellington? Will it make life easier for the airline staff working at the Mystery Weekend counter?

If an organisation is serious about its vision, it should measure every action and decision against it. If the proposed action doesn't fit with the vision or contribute to making it happen, it shouldn't be done.

Peter the Plumber wanted people to remember him. If changing the way he operated would make him less memorable, he wouldn't do it.

Mischief aimed to make shoe shopping fun. If a new policy would make the Mischief shopping experience less fun, they wouldn't do it.

If Mark was to succeed in translating the vision he'd articulated on the hustings into a workable plan for the city, the same discipline would have to apply in the council.

How to be a Top Town

A couple of months after the casino vote, Rachel once again approached Mark as he was warming down after a workout.

She'd been telling another of her clients about Mark and slippers and how the concept had led him to vote against the casino. Wellington had recently won the Top Town competition, having previously failed even to get on the shortlist. The client wondered if that achievement could be traced back to slippers. It was a good question, but Rachel had to say she'd get back to him. So, Mark: did it?

Impressed and delighted that Rachel had understood and embraced slippers to the extent that she was now spreading the word, Mark was happy to explain how the concept had given the city the critical winning edge that secured the Top Town award.

First morning as mayor

It had all started the morning after the election. Feeling pretty good about life, Mark left his inner-city apartment to buy a newspaper and a carton of milk from his local superette. As he was counting out the coins, the superette owner emerged from the back of the shop full of excitement. 'Hey Mark, congratulations,' he yelled in a voice that could have been heard a block away. 'You did it. You're the mayor of Wellington. How does it feel? We're proud of you, mate. You're going to turn this place upside down.' The man's delight was heart-warming, but his assumption that Mark was going to take the city by storm and transform it was slightly worrying. Mark hoped he could live up to his expectations.

A little later he strolled over to the Town Hall. The working day wasn't yet under way so it was empty and silent, which had the effect of making it more imposing. He sidled into the Council Chambers and approached the engraved mayoral chair that took pride of place at the top of the table. He couldn't resist the temptation to try it out so with a furtive glance over his shoulder he lowered the mayoral buttocks into the mayoral chair for the first time. It wasn't nearly as comfortable as it looked.

He registered the trappings of the Council Chamber — the flags, the tally board where votes were recorded, the

reassuringly solid furniture and the portraits of previous mayors, all of whom, so it seemed at that moment, were looking down their noses at him. It was a bit intimidating.

Having absorbed the atmosphere and sense of history of the chamber, Mark checked out his office. It was spacious, sunny and had a stunning view of the harbour. There was a huge mahogany desk with another very impressive chair which looked as if it had been designed for the posterior of a High Court judge or Speaker of the House rather than a shoe salesman. The in-tray was stacked high with official documents. It was like being given homework on the very first day of school.

The council chief executive knocked and entered.

'Your Worship.'

Once Mark realised she was talking to him, he decided he could get used to being called 'Your Worship'. It just seemed so right somehow.

'Congratulations on your election success.'

Pleasantries over, she asked him a question that, on the surface, was innocuously routine but actually put him on notice that there wouldn't be a honeymoon or settling-in period. It was, in fact, a polite way of telling him that reality was about to bite.

'Your Worship, what would you like the organisation you

now lead to do? There's a council meeting in three weeks and I'm sure you'd like to have some input into the work plan.'

 will end in tears'

His detractors expected Mark's mayoralty to start falling apart at this point. While he was an accomplished salesman and had proved to be an effective campaigner, they simply didn't think anyone with zero experience of politics or local government could run a city.

He hadn't been a councillor. In fact, he'd never shown any interest in being one.

The last meeting he'd chaired was held in a tree house in his parents' backyard.

How on earth would he lead a diverse and combative group of councillors in what was shaping up to be a challenging period for the city?

The sceptics shook their heads. The people of Wellington were going to learn the hard way that you should think very carefully before entrusting your city to a novice with no relevant experience. This was all going to end in tears.

It didn't work out that way.

Why are we here?

The vision — 'Send Yourself to Wellington' — was clear and simple and therefore powerful. Wellington would become a city that people loved to live in and looked forward to visiting. It most definitely wouldn't be a source of angst at the Mystery Weekend counter.

Mark was aware that many companies and organisations had developed visions which hadn't really achieved anything or made a difference.

There were various reasons why visions, having been introduced with great fanfare or solemnity, left people cold and failed to generate staff buy-in or a sense of ownership. Some visions were couched in such high-falutin language or were so vague and woolly that people within the organisation couldn't relate to them. Some were so long no one could remember them, let alone make a personal connection.

For that reason, he resisted pressure from council officers to produce a three-page vision statement. That sort of document wasn't going to make a difference. In fact, it would inhibit progress by over-complicating the issue. They'd end up as drops in the great sea of paper.

What the plumber taught the mayor about business

One small step

During a planning meeting with his management team, Mark illustrated the dangers of over-complicating a vision by telling an old story about the National Aeronautics and Space Administration (NASA) during the space race with the Soviet Union. NASA had brought in consultants to assist with a comprehensive review of operations intended to identify what the organisation could do better and how:

> The consultants decided that the first order of business was to establish what the purpose of NASA actually was. Unusually for consultants, they sought to find out by asking the people who worked there. The question they asked was: 'Why are you here?'
>
> The engineers' response was: 'We're responsible for people's lives and many millions of dollars worth of machinery. Our job is to ensure the machinery operates at optimal efficiency and safety.'
>
> The Human Resources department came back with this answer: 'Our role is to ensure that NASA hires the best people, pays its staff on time and complies with the legislative requirements relating to employment.'

Slippers: Service and Selling

The Research and Development team gave an array of answers. One group was working on a process to make rockets go faster for longer. Another was trying to create a more efficient propellant and the consultants simply didn't have a clue what the third group was up to. They appeared to be speaking a foreign language.

A pattern was emerging. Every team within the organisation was too focused on their specific task to think about the big picture. They couldn't see the woods for the trees. After talking to people in each department and at every level, the consultants were none the wiser as to what NASA's overall purpose was. Without that understanding, it was going to be very difficult to fit all the pieces together in a way that everyone in the organisation could understand and relate to.

Feeling like they were banging their heads against a brick wall, the dispirited consultants gathered for a cup of coffee and a debrief in the NASA cafeteria. It was deserted except for a janitor fixing a light. One of the consultants pointed out that they hadn't talked to any maintenance staff. The response from his colleagues was essentially, 'Be our guest.'

When the light was fixed the consultant wandered

over to ask the janitor if he'd mind answering a couple of questions about NASA. 'Sure,' said the janitor, 'as long as it won't take too long.' The consultant asked him: 'Why are you here?'

The janitor thought about it for a couple of seconds. 'To put a man on the moon,' he said, 'and bring him back safely.' The consultant stared at him, astonished.

'Is that it?' said the janitor. 'I'm kind of busy.' When the dumbstruck consultant nodded, the janitor hurried off to his next job.

The council management team nodded in unison. They got the point. The next step would be getting them to recognise that their organisation suffered from exactly the same problem.

Permeating every pore of an organisation

Developing and implementing a vision isn't an easy task as many organisations have discovered to their cost in terms of wasted time and effort. Without action, a vision is just a slogan and a pretty hollow one at that. The challenge is to ensure the vision permeates through the organisation. Everyone needs to understand it, buy into it and make a personal commitment to it.

Mark had learnt that lesson through the Mischief Guarantee. If the staff hadn't had a sense of ownership and taken such pride in it, it wouldn't have been a success.

Each month the council held orientation days for new staff. Time was always blocked off in Mark's diary to enable him to attend orientation in order to meet and chat with the new employees.

He would begin by welcoming them and thanking them for choosing to work at the council, and go on to outline in broad terms what the council did and what its short-term priorities were. Pretty standard stuff.

Then he'd introduce the slippers theme and talk about Peter's vision of being the plumbing outfit that people remembered and the Mischief vision of making shoe shopping fun. Finally, he threw in the airline stewardesses and his vision of people being delighted when their envelopes contained a ticket to Wellington.

By this stage of proceedings, without fail, there'd be a lot of nodding, accompanied by murmurs of assent and snatches of laughter. People understood where he was coming from. And having captured his audience, Mark would then hit them with what he regarded as the most important statement in his presentation:

'Do me a favour: if you find you don't like it here at the council, please leave.'

It would be greeted, without fail, with stunned silence. In fact, the first time Mark said it, the senior staff and HR people who were present were just as gobsmacked as the newcomers. Where did he get off saying something like that to new employees?

The explanation

Having got their attention, Mark went on to explain his bombshell: 'When people don't want to be at work, they can't hide the fact. It really shows: there's no energy, no fizz, and even without trying to be disruptive, they bring the people around them down. So my suggestion is this: if you don't like it here, don't stick around. I don't say that out of a deep concern for your personal happiness. My concern is to protect the positive atmosphere we've got here.'

In the pregnant hush that always followed this challenge, Mark half expected someone to say, 'Tell us what you really think.' No one ever did, although it was obvious that most people weren't used to having it laid on the line quite as bluntly as that. But after he'd followed up with an example, people usually got the point he was trying to make.

The example

Early in his mayoral term, Mark took a phone call from an older resident named Mrs Ramsey. She had something to say, but it was for the mayor's ears only: she steadfastly refused to talk to anyone else.

Mark took the call aware that it would be some sort of complaint, but in the dark as to the exact nature of it. The conversation went along these lines:

Mark: Hello, Mark here. How can I help?
Mrs Ramsey:
You can help by putting me through to

the mayor. I told the receptionist I wasn't prepared to talk to anyone else.

Mark: You're talking to the mayor. This is Mark Blumsky. I'm sorry to hear you've had a problem — why don't you tell me about it?

Mrs Ramsey:
Oh, well . . . Thank you, Mister Mayor. I was mentally prepared to spend the afternoon being fobbed off from one bureaucrat to another. Well, the reason for my call is this: I was in my little car today, going to see my baby granddaughter, when one of your great big rubbish trucks just pulled out in front of me with no warning whatsoever. I'm seventy-four years old and my reactions aren't what they used to be so I very nearly smashed straight into it.

Mark: That's no good. Are you sure it was a council truck?

Mrs Ramsey:
Well, it had your logo and 'Wellington City Council' in great big letters on the side.

Mark: That's pretty conclusive. Did you get the licence plate?

Mrs Ramsey:
> No, I was too busy beeping.

Mark: I don't blame you. What sort of response did that get?

Mrs Ramsey:
> Well, I'm very glad you asked. The driver wound down his window, put his arm out and made an extremely rude gesture. I mean, do you think ratepayers should have to put up with that sort of behaviour from city council employees?

Mark didn't think so at all. In fact, he was mortified. The truck driver had shown a reckless disregard for other people and compounded that with his contemptuous dismissal of Mrs Ramsey's absolutely justified protest.

And having copped that treatment, it was entirely understandable that Mrs Ramsey wanted to let the boss — Mark — know exactly how she felt about his organisation — the city council. She had every right to do so.

Perhaps the driver had had a row with his wife that morning or perhaps he was feeling unwell. Mrs Ramsey couldn't be expected to know that, any more than she could be expected to know his star sign. All she knew about the bloke was that he behaved badly behind the wheel of a truck covered in Wellington City Council signage. He obviously cared so little about the organisation he worked for that he didn't give two hoots about the consequences of his actions — the damage done to the council's image and reputation.

This sort of frankness made some people uncomfortable, but most took it in the spirit in which it was meant. Afterwards new staff members would frequently approach Mark with similar tales from their previous workplaces of low morale and image problems caused by colleagues who didn't care or simply didn't want to be there.

Working late

Three months after the casino vote, Mark was working late in his office, catching up on paperwork. Before shutting down his computer, he checked his in-box.

There were a number of e-mails, forwarded by Rachel, from members of a community group she belonged to. The group had been struggling with membership and funding and, at Mark's prompting, Rachel had stepped up to take a leadership role. Judging from the e-mails, she was having a galvanising effect. Clearly, her message about the importance of vision, points of difference and having a positive attitude had struck a chord. Virtually every e-mail referred to the group's determination to find their slippers and make a difference for the people in their community. In the space of a few months Rachel had gone from being a complete sceptic to an enthusiastic follower of the gospel according to Peter the Plumber and his offsider, Mark the Shoe Salesman.

'I've been wondering about that sign...'

As Mark prepared to call it a night, the regular cleaner Brian came in to vacuum the office and empty the rubbish bins as he did every night.

Brian often made a point of telling Mark that he was the fourth mayor he'd cleaned for and certainly one of the tidiest. That night, though, there was something else he wanted to talk about. He pointed to the sign stuck to the top right corner of Mark's computer screen:

Don't forget your slippers!

'I've been wondering about that sign,' said Brian. 'Are you planning to start sleeping in here? Don't you have a home to go to?'

Mark replied that if he didn't get the hell out of there soon, it would hardly be worth going home but, no, it had nothing to do with keeping his tootsies warm when he worked late. There was a long story behind the sign, but it would have to wait for another night: he was out of there. Brian nodded and got on with the vacuuming.

When Mark recalled the conversation later, he felt a pang of guilt. Given that Brian had plucked up the courage to ask, he knew he should really have told him the full story there and then. After all, once a month he trotted it out for new staff members so it was a bit unfair not to share it with poor old Brian who'd been around for so long he was part of the Town Hall furniture. Besides, Brian might even find the story useful. It had certainly had a positive effect on Rachel.

This train of thought led him to the realisation that Brian was in the same boat as all the long-serving members of staff: he hadn't told any of them about slippers and his vision for Wellington. He'd been so concerned with getting the message across to new employees, he'd overlooked the bulk of council staff. That was an oversight he'd have to correct in a hurry.

Next time Mark saw Brian, the cleaner was entering his office as he was racing out. Even though the timing was bad, he backtracked and asked Brian if he still wanted to know the story behind the sign. 'Very much so' was the reply. Mark sat him down and told him the story of the plumber and his slippers and how the lessons from that single encounter had exercised a profound influence on his subsequent career in business and politics.

Brian seemed to enjoy the story, but Mark was now running late for a family gathering so there was no time to discuss it further.

Smelling like roses

The following day Mark flew off to attend a conference on local government wastewater treatment issues — he'd been looking forward to it for months — and a week would pass before he returned to his office.

The moment he set foot in there he knew that something had changed. He couldn't put his finger on it, but something was definitely different. It wasn't until he'd spent ten minutes going around his office like a detective examining a crime scene that the penny dropped: the change wasn't visible; it was in the air. His office smelt different. It didn't smell like commercial cleaning product, that faintly antiseptic smell we associate with public buildings. The new smell was floral. It was almost as if his office had been relocated to the Botanic Gardens.

He asked his assistant about the new fragrance. It was nothing to do with her, she said, but she could confirm that all the offices on their floor now smelt more like roses than Dettol and the staff seemed very happy about it. A couple of people had asked her who had authorised the change, but she couldn't shed any light on the matter, apart from the fact that she'd first noticed the new smell about a week earlier.

The obvious person to ask was Brian, so next time Mark was in his office when the cleaner came in, he put it on him: did Brian have anything to do with this mysterious fragrance which was getting the thumbs up from everyone on the floor? Almost bashfully, Brian revealed that he was using a new room-freshening spray:

> 'I took on board the message from your story. I realised that I didn't have any slippers. I left a room clean but it looked and smelt like every room in

every professionally cleaned building in town. I was working hard, but there was nothing special about what I was doing.

'So that weekend I went shopping with my wife and we tried every single room-freshening spray on the shelves. We picked the one that we both thought was the nicest and that's what I'm using now when I finish up in a room. It costs a bit more than the standard stuff, but I reckon it's worth it. From what I hear it's gone down pretty well so I'm glad I made the effort. You could say I've found my slippers.'

Mark shook Brian's hand and congratulated him on a great initiative. The next day he went out of his way to spread the word that the staff had Brian to thank for making their workplace more pleasant.

We should celebrate whenever a person or organisation or city finds their slippers.